Democracy's Double-Edged Sword

Democracy's Double-Edged Sword

*How Internet Use Changes Citizens' Views
of Their Government*

CATIE SNOW BAILARD

Johns Hopkins University Press

Baltimore

© 2014 Johns Hopkins University Press
All rights reserved. Published 2014
Printed in the United States of America on acid-free paper
9 8 7 6 5 4 3 2 1

Johns Hopkins University Press
2715 North Charles Street
Baltimore, Maryland 21218-4363
www.press.jhu.edu

Library of Congress Cataloging-in-Publication Data

Bailard, Catie Snow.
   Democracy's double-edged sword : how Internet use changes citizens' views of their
government / Catie Snow Bailard.
      pages cm
   Includes bibliographical references and index.
   ISBN 978-1-4214-1525-3 (paperback) — ISBN 978-1-4214-1526-0 (electronic)
— ISBN 1-4214-1525-9 (paperback) 1. Political participation—Technological
innovations. 2. Decision making—Citizen participation—Technological innovations.
3. Public administration—Citizen participation—Technological innovations. 4. Public
administration—Public opinion. 5. Internet—Political aspects. 6. Digital media—Political
aspects. 7. Democracy. 8. Democratization. 9. Comparative government. I. Title.
   JF799.5.B35 2014
   323'.04202854678—dc23   2014006748

A catalog record for this book is available from the British Library.

*Special discounts are available for bulk purchases of this book. For more information,
please contact Special Sales at 410-516-6936 or specialsales@press.jhu.edu.*

Johns Hopkins University Press uses environmentally friendly book materials,
including recycled text paper that is composed of at least 30 percent post-consumer
waste, whenever possible.

To my family

CONTENTS

ACKNOWLEDGMENTS

There is no greater advantage for an academic than having learned from great teachers and been mentored by world-class scholars. I am enormously indebted to those who have contributed to my education and professional development over the years and grateful for the thoughtful feedback I have received from a phenomenal set of colleagues and peers.

Starting with my early school years, I would like to thank Sally Durham, Lauren Newington, Gary Dalton, Carla Newton, Lori Lambertson, Steve Smuin, Emily White, Leanne Rouser, Barbara Callahan, and Russ Kubiak.

Moving to my graduate student years, I want to thank James DeNardo, Jeff Lewis, Dan Posner, Richard Rosecrance, and Tom Schwartz. And a special thank-you to Matt Baum, Tim Groeling, Lynn Vavreck, and John Zaller. I feel incredibly fortunate to have been mentored by such accomplished and brilliant academics. I would particularly like to acknowledge my chair, Matt Baum, for his continuing mentorship. From sound advice, insightful feedback, and unceasing encouragement and belief in my work—it would be impossible to express my gratitude for all of the effort, time, and guidance you have provided me throughout the years.

Over the course of the (many) years that I have worked on the research contributing to this book, I have benefited from the feedback of a number of esteemed colleagues and peers. A big thank-you to Bob Entman, Ryan Enos, Seth Hill, Matt Hindman, Phil Howard, Dave Karpf, Brian Law, Steve Livingston, James Lo, Phil Potter, John Sides, and Nikki Usher. In particular, I would like to acknowledge the tireless support of Kim Gross, one of the best senior colleagues a junior faculty member could hope for.

I am grateful to the many translators and research assistants who have helped me along the way: Cara Bumgardner, Melissa and Mirza Delibegovic, Todd Kominiak, Jake Miller, and Flora and Fulgence Mishili. Thank-you as well to the organizations that provided funding for this research: the UCLA Communication Department's Edward A. Dickson Graduate Research Fellowship and George Washington University's Office of the Vice President of Research.

I thank the reviewers of this book, whose feedback and astute suggestions strengthened it markedly. And, a big thank-you to Suzanne Flinchbaugh and everyone at Johns Hopkins University Press involved with the publication of this book; I appreciate your support and effort throughout this process.

Finally, I would like to acknowledge my parents, Terri and Tom Bailard. Thank you for instilling me with a solid work ethic and an unyielding appreciation for learning. It is from you both that I have learned the most.

Democracy's Double-Edged Sword

CHAPTER 1

Why the Effect of Internet Use on Political Evaluations Matters

D EMONSTRATIONS RANGING from Wall Street and London to the Middle East, North Africa, and China have focused global attention on the Internet's capacity to facilitate political organization by disaffected citizens. As the Internet's role in such protests grows increasingly prominent, the time-honored debate over whether advances in information and communication technology will beget democratic gains has reignited, with the loudest voices ringing from the newest generation of technological optimists and skeptics.

This book explores a related, equally important, yet largely understudied component of the Internet's potential to facilitate prodemocratic behavior. Specifically, to what degree does Internet use influence citizens' desire to act or organize politically in the first place? While it is clearly important to understand how Internet use can streamline political organization once people are moved to action, less attention has been paid to whether Internet use influences citizens at this more foundational, antecedent stage of political action.

Accordingly, this book examines the Internet's influence on citizens' evaluations of their government's performance, particularly whether the Internet influences their satisfaction regarding the quality of democratic practices available in their nation. The impetus to act politically—from day-to-day civic activities to the more extreme cases of protest and revolution—begins in the minds of men and women. In this vein, I argue that Internet use meaningfully alters not only the quantity and range of information but also the criteria through which individuals evaluate their governments—shaping their evaluations and satisfaction accordingly. I will show that Internet use has a contingent effect on satisfaction with the quality of democratic practices available in one's own nation: whereas Internet use will increase satisfaction in advanced democracies, it will depress satisfaction in nations with weak democratic practices.

This is an important consideration, since it is these evaluations that can and will encourage men and women to act and organize toward political ends. It is clearly useful, then, to understand the influence of Internet use on citizens' evaluations in countries that are democratizing as well as those that are in full democracies. After all, these governments and their constitutions are primarily predicated on the principles of accountability and responsiveness. In representative democracies, for example, citizens vote for those candidates whom they believe will best represent their own interests. Once elected, those officials are entrusted with making decisions about the salient issues and policies of the day in a manner that promotes their constituents' well-being. Information about the activities of these elected officials, therefore, is a primary determinant of citizens' evaluations of how well officials are actually performing the job they were elected to do. When officials fail to meet these expectations, opponents can capitalize on citizens' dissatisfaction to unseat the incumbent.

It is also instructive to consider the impact of Internet use on evaluations and satisfaction in nondemocratic countries. One may be inclined to ask: What does it matter how citizens evaluate the quality of democratic practices and more general governmental processes in decidedly nondemocratic nations where the channels for citizens' evaluations to influence the decisions of government officials have traditionally been highly constrained? But consider the fact that many nations—even ostensibly nondemocratic countries—entertain some limited degree of democratic practices. For example, each of the seventy-three countries in this analysis holds some form of regular elections of government officials. After all, elections are a rather effective mechanism for governments to make grand gestures demonstrating that they are responsive to their citizens' interests and well-being. Even better, when the votes are counted and the incumbent party or official has carried the ballot box, what better means is there of validating that incumbent's mandate as the appropriate and rightful leader of its citizens?

Of course, in some cases these elections do not amount to much more than an exercise in futility, with the outcome already well determined by the ruling party regardless of what the ballots say. However, while outsiders may take for granted that many of these elections are largely shams, citizens of these countries often place value in these elections. Consider the buildup to the Egyptian revolution of 2011, during which soon-to-be protesters, originally mobilized by police brutality, were further incensed by ostensibly rigged parliamentary elections—eyewitness accounts and even video of which were uploaded and documented online in the months leading up to the protests.

In this vein, Levitsky and Way (2002) note the proliferation and staying power in recent decades of hybrid regimes that pair authoritarian governance with democratic rules. These regimes, which they term *competitive authoritarianism,* integrate formal democratic institutions as the principal means of obtaining and exercising political authority. But they fail to meet conventional minimum standards for democracy such as free and fair elections, universal adult suffrage, and the protection of human rights and political liberties.

According to Levitsky and Way, although governments in these states often violate democratic practices, they tend not to openly flout certain democratic practices, thanks to the presence of some rather durable democratic institutions in these countries—institutions that the citizens value and have a vested interest in protecting. Thus, authoritarian governments can coexist with democratic institutions as long as incumbents avoid egregious human rights abuses and do not openly thwart elections. This creates a dilemma for incumbents, who must determine how far they can subvert or manipulate these institutions to preserve their own power without provoking widespread attention, dissatisfaction, and reprisal.

Not surprisingly, the contradictory features characterizing these regimes are an inherent source of instability—an instability that has only grown since the introduction of the Internet as the regimes' control over the flows of information within and across their borders wanes. In the Internet age, it is simply more difficult for these governments to control information in order to mask their violations of human rights and established democratic institutions. This has multiple implications. The first is an increase in the likelihood that these transgressions will be exposed to public scrutiny and will elicit dissatisfaction from disaffected citizens. This translates into an increased motivation and capacity for citizens or challengers to mount campaigns to oust poorly performing governments either through election, protest, coup, or revolt. However, this dynamic also has implications for the more day-to-day evaluations that citizens make of their governments as well as for the incentives of incumbent governments to heed those evaluations. Thus, the impact of this altered incentive structure will manifest in even the mundane processes and everyday decisions of these governments in meaningful ways.

Accordingly, recent demonstrations across the globe illustrate how the Internet's capacity to promote dissatisfaction and encourage citizens to more critically evaluate poorly performing governments can have real and profound consequences in the short term. Beyond this, uncovering and testing how Internet use influences the information and criteria that individuals use to evaluate their governments will also provide a stronger foundation for predicting the long-term and more subtle effects of the Internet on the informational relationship shared by citizens and their governments as well as the day-to-day political implications of this changing relationship.

While many trumpet the democratic potential of the Internet, its effect is neither automatic nor uniform. One democratic gain, such as more critical evaluations of poorly performing governments, does not automatically set off a domino effect of entirely prodemocratic gains in citizens' attitudes and behaviors. For example, the field experiment conducted during Tanzania's 2010 presidential election (discussed in chapter 7) revealed that although the Internet equipped individuals with more robust information upon which to question the integrity of their election—thereby making these individuals more skeptical that the election and subsequent recount were conducted fairly—these disaffected Internet users also became less likely to vote. After all, the belief that an election is not being conducted fairly can produce two very divergent responses: some people may protest and take to the streets, while others may simply throw up their hands and stay home. Additionally, the field experiment in Bosnia and Herzegovina (discussed in chapter 6) showed that individuals who became more critical of the quality of democracy in their country after Internet use were also more likely to question whether the current democratic system was the right choice for their country. Taken as a whole, the research presented in this book shows that the Internet's influence is a complex, context-dependent process that in some instances will prove to be a double-edged sword for democracy and democratization. Thus, it appears that both the Internet's optimists and its skeptics likely have it partially right.

Mirror-Holding and Window-Opening

As a result of the sweeping changes in contemporary information landscapes ushered in by new information and communication technologies (ICT), information retrieval, dispersion, and archiving is facilitated via the Internet at levels unprecedented in the history of human civilization (described in more detail in chapter 2). This means that it is less costly in terms of time, effort, and resources for average citizens to receive and contribute information more quickly and in greater abundance than has ever before been possible. As a result of this massive decentralization of information and communication capacity, the Internet expands the set of information and alters the criteria upon which individuals evaluate their own governments, shaping their satisfaction accordingly.

Specifically, the influence of Internet use on individuals' evaluations and satisfaction travels through two primary avenues, which I term *mirror-holding* and *window-opening*. First, through mirror-holding, the Internet provides a larger and more diverse array of political information than the traditional media system could provide, enabling users to better discern and reflect on how democracy—and governance more generally—actually functions in their own country. Second, according to window-opening, the global nature of the Internet also opens a larger window for individuals to better view how governments function in other countries, particularly the advanced democracies that are most visible on the Internet. This provides users with a more realistic and globally consistent scale by which to make comparative evaluations about how well their own government functions. Taken together, these mechanisms suggest that the Internet has the potential to play a central role in shaping the evaluations and resultant satisfaction that citizens harbor toward their governments.

Relatedly, mirror-holding and window-opening also make control of information and communication much more costly and inefficient for all types of governments in the Internet age. As Larry Diamond notes, "With recent technological revolutions, the ability to generate information and opinion has been radically decentralized" (2008, 99). Philip N. Howard (2010) observes that whereas it was relatively efficient for states to control traditional media, and costly for citizens to have their voices heard through those systems, the Internet has flipped this equation on its head. Instead, it has become relatively efficient and cheap for citizens to disseminate information, and rather costly for governments to control that expression. This has potentially profound consequences for the set of information and criteria that citizens use to evaluate their governments.

Evaluations and their influence on satisfaction are foundational to the cost-benefit calculus that determines political activity, which predicts that individuals will engage in political behavior when the expected benefits brought by that act outweigh the perceived costs of the act. The poorer the evaluations of a government, the greater the dissatisfaction and the greater the perceived benefits of political action to effect political change. Thus, critical evaluations and dissatisfaction lower the point at which the expected benefits of political behavior outweigh the expected costs, increasing the likelihood that individuals will deem specific political acts worthwhile. More critical evaluations can also facilitate political organization by providing would-be mobilizers (both grassroots and elite) with a more motivated pool of citizens to appeal to more efficiently, who increasingly harbor a shared sense of a national "problem" and therefore also increasingly share a sense of need to redress that problem. Thus, according to this "instrumental view" of Internet effects, as termed by Bruce Bimber (2003), the Internet can alter the cost-benefit calculus of political behavior by lowering the costs of organization due to reduced communication costs. However, Internet use can also alter this cost-benefit calculus by providing citizens with information that makes them increasingly dissatisfied with the performance of their government.

The import of such evaluations to the calculus of political activity is borne out by empirical research, which shows that satisfaction with democracy is correlated with support for elected officials, support for the process of democratization itself, and citizens' preference for democracy (Baviskar & Malone 2004; Bratton & Mattes 2001; Clarke, Dutt, & Kornberg 1993; Sarsfield & Echegaray 2006). In nations transitioning to democracy, "the most significant predictors of support for democratic norms are how people evaluate democracy in practice" (Evans & Whitefield 1995, 512). On the other end, dissatisfaction with democracy contributes to support for regime change (Harmel & Robertson 1986). In support of both of these findings, Sarsfield and Echegary conclude that "satisfaction with democracy stimulates adherence to democracy. . . . Conversely, dissatisfaction with democracy visibly generates doubts or overt rejection of democracy" (2006, 159). Thus, satisfaction is a central determinant of citizens' willingness to stick with the circuitous and sometimes unpleasant process of democratization. Moreover, even in instances that fall well short of calls for regime change (dis)satisfaction can precipitate a range of potentially consequential political actions. Summarizing a range of scholarship, Lohmann (1993) concludes, "Major policy changes are often preceded by political action: people sign petitions, take part in demonstrations, or participate in violent riots to express their dissatisfaction with the status quo" (319).

The effect of Internet use on citizens' evaluations of their government also has implications for the more day-to-day decisions and processes of governments, even in instances that do not result in visible political organization or protest. Satisfaction is strongly associated with a range of evaluations that are integral to political attitudes and behavior. For example, research by Zmerli, Newton, and Montero (2007), demonstrates a close relationship shared by democratic satisfaction and political confidence, which is defined as "citizens' attitudes towards the core institutions and key actors of the political regime" (Denters et al. 2007, 67). The political import of this is illustrated by research that confirms the effect of institutional trust on a citizens' propensity to engage in a range of important political behaviors: "Citizens who are more trusting of political institutions are more likely to vote, follow politics, feel a sense of civic duty, and have high levels of political knowledge" (Mishler & Rose 2005, 19). Conversely, "Declining political trust contributes to this dissatisfaction, creating an environment in which it is difficult for those in government to succeed" (Hetherington 1998, 791).

More basically, governing is simply easier when officials control the information and communication that shape citizens' evaluations of their performance and thus their satisfaction. In illustration of this, Joseph Stiglitz advises: "Secrecy gives those in government exclusive control over certain areas of knowledge, and thereby increases their power. . . . Secrecy was the hallmark of the totalitarian states that marred the 20th century, yet even though the public may have an interest in openness, public officials have incentives to pursue secrecy even in democratic societies" (2002, 29–34). Functioning democracies have built-in mechanisms to guard against leaders' instinct to hoard information, such as freedom of the press, freedom of information, and institutionalized procedures to promote transparency (albeit a multitude of recent examples demonstrate that these mechanisms are often imperfect at best). Without such mechanisms, the leaders of democratizing and authoritarian governments are even freer to exploit the asymmetrical distribution of information and communication in their nations in order to engage in corrupt or self-serving behavior that is often directly at odds with the interests of their populations as a whole. Not only does control of information facilitate the actual acts of malfeasance, but it also minimizes the likely consequences of such behavior (in the form of remonstrations from opponents and international bodies as well as unrest and protests by citizens) by keeping would-be critics and citizens in the dark regarding the details and extent of such behavior.

In the Internet age, governments—democratic, democratizing, and non-democratic alike—are aware that they have lost some degree of control over information flows compared to what they enjoyed in the era of traditional broadcast media systems. As a result, they are aware that there is greater potential for their decisions and actions to be broadcast onto the national and even international stage in a venue and context over which they have diminished control. Without doubt, there are other means available to government officials to pursue corrupt or self-serving ends and to manage or suppress populations. But it is simply more efficient when government officials do not have to resort to more active and severe measures of suppression and repression. Thus, by controlling information from the outset, states enjoyed a greater capacity to coopt their citizens by influencing the set of information as well as the criteria and expectations that citizens draw upon to evaluate their performance—shaping their citizens' satisfaction accordingly.

This by no means suggests that governments are now entirely beholden to public opinion in the course of decision making in the Internet age, nor are they likely to see themselves as such. But governments are aware that they must, nevertheless, weight the potential activation of "latent public opinion"—a term first introduced by V. O. Key (1961)—in ways that they rarely had to previously. John Zaller aptly summarized latent public opinion as "opinion that might exist at some point in the future in response to the decision-makers' actions and may therefore result in political damage or even the defeat at the polls" (2002, 2).

Clearly, the potential activation of latent public opinion has direct implications for elected officials in democratic and democratizing countries; however, the growth and staying power of hybrid regimes means that latent public opinion is increasingly important to officials in nondemocratic countries as well. Essentially, with the massive decentralization of information and diminished control of gatekeepers in determining which information makes it onto the public stage (in democratic and nondemocratic states alike), elites have become less able to control which information is likely to become salient and, as a result, less able to predict the activation of latent public opinion.

This alters the decision-making calculus that guides governments' decisions—though not always for the better and sometimes subtly. Nevertheless, this means that the capacity for Internet use to alter the information and criteria that citizens use to evaluate their governments will exert an incremental but still meaningful influence on the day-to-day decisions of governments. Even in instances that fall short of precipitating visible political activity and protest, this altered decision-making calculus will have meaningful implications for the processes and policies that characterize governments in the Internet age. This also means that Internet use affects citizens' evaluations and satisfaction both directly and indirectly.

This is not to say that states will not try to monitor and limit the dissemination of information in the Internet age. Some governments remain committed to censoring the Internet in their nations. And some have achieved a fair degree of success doing so (Kalathil & Boas 2001, 2003). However, even in countries with the most successful of Internet regulatory systems, examples abound of instances in which critical information and communication slipped through the cracks.

In the following chapters, I develop the concepts of mirror-holding and window-opening more fully. But first, I want to provide two vivid examples of the meaningful ways that the Internet's mirror-holding and window-opening are changing the informational relationship between governments and their citizens as well as the potential consequences of this changing dynamic for citizens' evaluations and satisfaction.

A Tale of Two Chinese Earthquakes

In 1976 a 7.8-magnitude earthquake struck the Chinese province of Tang-shan. The central government remained unaware that the earthquake had even occurred until a coal miner drove an ambulance six hours to alert party leaders in their compound. Several more days passed before the government sent relief operations, and when rescuers finally did arrive, they were severely short-handed (Tyler 1995).

Although the state-run media noted the earthquake, its reports were brief and lacking in details. Citizens with loved ones in the region seeking information were rebuffed by the government, which, in the midst of political upheaval, sought to refocus national attention on their own agenda, announcing over state media: "There were merely several hundred thousand deaths. So what? Denouncing Deng concerns eight hundred million people" (Chang 2003, 493). In international media, the Chinese government was even more tight-lipped, refusing to admit the earthquake had occurred at all. To maintain this pretense, the government refused all offers of international aid. It was not until three years later that the Chinese government provided any concrete information to the international community regarding the earthquake at all (Tyler 1995).

Contrast this with the 7.9-magnitude earthquake suffered in China's Sichuan province in May 2008. Within minutes, news of the earthquake spread on the Internet. Within a week, individuals posted more than 200,000 blog posts (on three blogs alone) and nearly 5,000 videos pertaining to the earthquake (CIC 2008). This quickly dispersed detailed information about the earthquake throughout China and the world.

Netizens[1] used the Internet to determine the fate of missing loved ones, share news of the disaster, and help the government distribute relief. For example, a college student used a blog post to help the army locate a suitable field for landing a relief helicopter to rescue her family. Chinese netizens also monitored earthquake relief corruption via the Web, using it to identify and coordinate protests against suspected misappropriation of relief resources. Netizens also utilized the Internet to criticize the government for attempting to cover up the extent of the damage. In one such example, angry parents took to the Web to broadcast their suspicions regarding why so many schools collapsed while government buildings remained standing, calling international attention to the issue and pressing the government for an investigation.

This "relatively vigorous flow of information and the fast response from top officials and rescue workers stood in stark contrast to the way China handled the Tangshan Earthquake" (qtd. in Jeffries 2011, 25), which vividly illustrates the degree to which the Internet is altering the informational relationship between government officials and their citizens. Thanks to mirror-holding, the Internet dramatically expands the range and amount of information citizens receive about their own nations and their governments' activities. In addition to making it more efficient for citizens to access this information, the Internet enables those same citizens to contribute their own observations and voices to this informational landscape. Thus, the mirror provided by the Internet reflects back to citizens a more nuanced, broader, and more accurate picture of how their government is actually performing the task of governance—in this instance, how effectively it carried out relief and rescue efforts—than the traditional media could provide.

The Internet also amplifies the speed and ease with which information crosses borders—as window-opening contends—so that by 2008, refusing international aid would have been nearly as difficult for the Chinese government as denying the earthquake had occurred at all. Not only does information about one's own nation diffuse more readily across borders—such as the angry parents who used the Internet to call international attention to the faulty school buildings—but the Internet also exposes individuals to more information about other nations. This is important because it means that Internet use can alter the criteria and expectations that individuals draw upon to evaluate their own governments.

For example, how many Chinese citizens, disgruntled with their government's response to the 2008 earthquake, were previously exposed to information about how foreign governments—and their citizens—responded to their own natural disasters, such as Hurricane Katrina in the United States in 2005 or the floods in South Asia in 2007? Moreover, the capacity for window-opening to encourage comparative evaluations of one's own government with the performance of other governments can take both contemporaneous and retrospective views. In this case, Japan's 8.9-magnitude earthquake in 2011 elicited a new round of evaluations by Chinese citizens comparing the quality of their own government's earthquake preparedness and recovery efforts in 2008 to that of Japan's response three years later:

Despite its long-running feud with its neighbor, many Chinese respect both the way Japan has prepared for natural disasters and how it responds to them. . . . In the 2008 Sichuan earthquake several thousand school buildings collapsed, killing thousands of children and bringing the world's attention to the shoddy "tofu-dregs" buildings and rampant corruption that had skimmed the public funds earmarked for their construction. In Japan, on the other hand, schools must be designed to withstand sustained shaking. . . . Therefore, when photographs were posted of children as well as adults seeking shelter at schools in Friday's earthquake, people in China were reminded of how tens of thousands of Chinese students might have been saved. (*Want China Times* 2011)

The Arab Spring

Most visibly, Egypt's revolution showcased the Internet's capacity to serve as a tool for political organization during the massive protests that engulfed Egypt for three weeks and forced the ouster of President Hosni Mubarak after a 30-year reign. However, it is important not to overlook the role that the Internet played in the months leading up to the protests by fomenting, or at least focusing, the discontent that eventually fueled the movement.

Any consideration of this necessarily begins with Khaled Said, an Egyptian businessman and activist who was literally pulled from an Internet café and publicly beaten to death by two police officers in June of 2010. His crime? Disseminating video footage online of police officers engaged in corrupt acts. After his death, an anonymous human rights group created the Facebook page "We are all Khaled Said," which posted mobile phone pictures of his bruised and battered face in the morgue to call attention to this injustice and to provide a venue for public discussion of the inhumane treatment of Egyptians by their government (Preston 2011). Within weeks, 130,000 members joined the page, and by the time the movement began in earnest, this number had grown to more than 380,000 (*Frontline* 2011). During the protests that gripped Egypt for nearly three weeks, this page continued to serve as a central platform for organizing and sustaining protest activities.

However, the question remains: to what degree was Facebook and the Internet more generally a central or necessary tool for marshaling public sentiment in the months leading up to the movement? From a scientist's perspective, this question is impossible to answer definitively—first and foremost, due to the lack of a counterfactual. It is simply not possible to empirically prove Internet use played an imperative role in fomenting the discontent that ultimately resulted in the ouster of President Mubarak, because it is impossible to compare this outcome to that which would have occurred in a world without the Internet.

Nevertheless, it is clear that individuals central to this protest consider the Internet a crucial factor in the months leading up to the protests. Wael Ghonim—prominent activist, Google executive, and later-revealed administrator of the "We are all Khaled Said" Facebook page—said in an interview with CBS's *60 Minutes* (2011) after his 12-day incarceration by the Egyptian government, "If there was no social networks, it would have never been sparked. Because the whole thing before the revolution was the most critical thing. Without Facebook, without Twitter, without Google, without YouTube, this would have never happened."

This case provides a vivid illustration of how the Internet's mirror-holding and window-opening functions provide information that meaningfully and consequentially influence citizens' evaluations and satisfaction. First, Facebook served as a shared, visible, and publicly accessible repository of citizens' experience with police brutality. This mirror aggregated and centralized information for public consumption regarding the extent and magnitude of police brutality in Egypt. In the coming months, this page would also provide details (including eyewitness videos and photos) of election-rigging and more general instances of government corruption. This had a meaningful effect on individuals' understanding of the degree to which the Egyptian government was violating human rights and established democratic institutions—the very institutions that Levitsky and Way (2002) warn authoritarian governments not to flout too openly if they want to keep their jobs.

Of course, this is not to say that the Egyptian citizens were previously unaware of the existence of police brutality and corruption in their nation. However, there is a difference between awareness of the experiences suffered by yourself and those close to you, stories of malfeasance and brutality that you happen to catch wind of, and the manner in which the Internet's mirror visibly documents and aggregates these experiences at a national level. By providing an online venue for citizens to publicly document government abuses, often coupled with pictures and videos, individuals could more readily link their personal experiences to a much larger, more pervasive, and entrenched national trend. Thus, as Hossam El Hamalawy, the executive director of the Cairo Institute for Human Rights Studies, portended nearly a year before the protests began, "In the past few years, this issue of police torture has been highlighted in a way that was not highlighted before. . . . When people now get tortured, they speak about it. The public perception of what's to be done about police torture is changing" (qtd. in Chick 2010).

The significance of the capacity for citizens to document and aggregate instances of bad governance on a national scale through mirror-holding is reflected in Kinder and Kiewiet's (1981) study of sociotropic voting. This study revealed that (contrary to the then-prevailing scholarly view) when deciding how to cast their vote, voters were more likely to take into account the nation's overall economic health rather than their own personal economic well-being. To explain this, they note work by political scientist Robert E. Lane (1962), which finds that people "morselize" their private experience: "[T]he events and details of daily life are typically not interpreted as instances of broader themes, political or otherwise. . . . Such morselization is an enormous obstacle to the politicization of private experience"; on the other hand, "information about national conditions is typically conveyed at a level of abstraction appropriate to nationally-oriented political judgments" (Kinder and Kiewiet, 1981, 158).

Thus, by serving as a public venue to document and visibly aggregate the extent of government failure and malfeasance in a way that had never before been possible in these countries, exposure to this information online makes personal experiences less likely to be morselized. Instead, the mirror provided by the Internet encourages individuals to link their own grievances and experiences to a larger, more entrenched, and pervasive national trend—shaping their evaluations and satisfaction with their government accordingly. In the case of Egypt, by serving as a public venue to catalogue and graphically illustrate citizens' personal experiences, the Internet conveyed to Egyptian citizens a powerful picture of the full extent of entrenched corruption and brutality in their nation.

In addition to heightening the Egyptian population's sense of anger and dissatisfaction, this mirror also served to engender a shared sense of a pressing need to redress this systemic failure of their incumbent government. Not only did the Internet provide citizens with more information regarding the actual extent of corruption and malfeasance perpetrated by their government, but it also provided individuals with more information about their fellow citizens by better reflecting back to them the full extent and intensity of shared public anger. In support of this, Howard and Hussain (2011) observe, "Such media were singularly powerful in spreading protest messages. . . . connecting frustrated citizens with one another, and helping them to realize that they could take shared action regarding shared grievances."

Thus, not only does mirror-holding document and aggregate information about government failure at a level of abstraction that is conducive to broadening the sense of dissatisfaction shared across a population, but it also helps relay signals between fed-up citizens that they are not alone or even in the minority. This better enables individuals to overcome the fear that had previously rendered them inactive by signaling that they will not be the only ones willing to act—making it more likely (but by no means inevitable) that citizens will be able to overcome the key challenge to potentially dangerous political collective action identified by Kricheli, Livne, and Managoli: "who would be brave enough to take the first move" (2011, 31).

In Egypt, the Internet provided information that made it clear that individuals' anger was broadly shared, and thus the costs of standing up to the government would not be borne by only a few but instead distributed over a large group. This is supported by on-the-ground research during the protests, which found that "people learned about the protests primarily through interpersonal communication using Facebook. . . . Controlling for other factors, social media use greatly increased the odds that a respondent attended protests on the first day" (Tufekci & Wilson 2012).

Finally, let us return to the picture of Khaled Said's battered corpse in the morgue, as well as the death of Mohammed Bouazizi, the grocer in Tunisia who set himself on fire in front of a municipal building in protest of the humiliation and extortion he had suffered at the hands of a policewoman. In a recent BBC piece, M. Almond (2011) notes: "Violent death has been the most common catalyst for radicalising discontent in the revolutions of the last 30 years. Sometimes the spark is grisly. . . . Sometimes the desperate act of a single suicidally inflammatory protester . . . catches the imagination of a country." While violent death has long been a catalyst for uprisings, consider how the effect of violent death is magnified in the Internet age. Previously, news of such brutality traveled mouth-to-mouth through verbal descriptions and accounts. Now the mirror provided by the Internet means that pictures of the mutilated corpse and bereaved loved ones—if not images of the killing itself—can be uploaded for instantaneous documentation and distribution. While it is one thing to hear a grisly account of the unfair death of a citizen at the hands of his or her government, it is quite another to see it with one's own eyes. Images communicate visceral and emotional information regarding the true human costs of police brutality or an unjust government that words cannot as readily convey.

The international exchange of information enabled by the Internet also had several window-opening consequences for the Egyptian revolution. Most visibly, the success of the protests was likely helped by the fact that the world was watching—binding the hands of the Egyptian government to some degree and preventing more severe means of retaliation that government officials likely would have preferred if no one was watching. It is also clear that the Internet sent strong signals to the protesters about the degree of international support that they could expect. This was evident on the Facebook page with accounts of rallies in support of Egyptian protesters taking place in other countries, statements of support from foreign leaders, as well as non-Egyptian Facebook users directly expressing their support through comments and pictures posted to the page. Then, as protests spread throughout and beyond Egypt, organization efforts were further facilitated by the use of the Internet to learn about and adopt the protest techniques already demonstrated in other countries.

Consider also the Internet's more subtle effect in the months leading up to the Egyptian revolution. The Internet provided direct exposure to the difference between what Egyptians endured and what citizens living in developed democracies experienced. It also illustrated the shared failings of other nondemocratic states in terms of the degree to which these governments failed to promote and protect their own citizens' well-being. Thus, while domestic information regarding the Egyptian government's abuses meant that personal experiences were no longer morselized but were embedded in a larger national trend, exposure to the performance of other democratic and nondemocratic governments facilitated the realization that theirs was not a singular national experience but a shared dysfunction of the regime type. "This generation's access to a life without borders through the Internet and pan-Arab television networks like Al Jazeera exposed them to other societies, fueling anger at the repressive politics and economic stagnation that deprived the region's youth of opportunity and freedom" (Slackman 2011). Thus, Diamond's observation regarding the significance of exposure to governance and political activity in other countries as a powerful force for the diffusion of democratic values in previous waves of democratization is perhaps even more significant in the Internet age: "As news spread of nearly universal authoritarian dysfunction and corruption, people living under an authoritarian regime placed their national experiences within a wider context. . . . Authoritarianism had failed as a system" (2008, 111).

In summary, Internet use played an integral role in the months and weeks leading up to these revolutions—altering both the set of information Egyptians used to evaluate their own government and the criteria and expectations that shaped those evaluations. The resulting dissatisfaction and mounting anger set the stage for protest and revolution. In the cases of Egypt and Tunisia, the protests successfully ended decades of rule by corrupt regimes. And in the following months, the Internet continued to play an integral role in these nations as the interim governments and political activists struggled to build a framework for functioning democratic governance. But, reflecting the theme that emerges throughout the research presented in this book, the capacity for the Internet to effect one prodemocratic set of changes—such as the ouster of a dictator by popular protests—by no means sets off a chain of inevitably prodemocratic developments. Instead, as the events unfolding in Egypt compellingly demonstrate, the Internet as a force for democratization is most likely to prove a double-edged sword.

How This Book Diverges from and Contributes to the Current Body of Research

Departing from the bulk of extant research in this discipline, this book does not focus on the country-level correlation between ICT diffusion and democratization, nor does it consider its effect on the political activities of individuals or the organizational processes of political groups or institutions. Rather, it explores the Internet's influence at a more fundamental level: How does the Internet influence individuals' satisfaction with their government's performance as well as their related evaluations and expectations? This is an important component of the Internet's potential to encourage political behavior, since it is these evaluations and expectations that drive citizens to act or organize in the first place. By better understanding how the Internet influences individuals at this most basic and antecedent level, we will be in a better position to predict when dissatisfaction and more critical evaluations will encourage individuals to act and organize.

This analysis also provides insight into the meaningful influence the Internet exerts on the informational relationship between governments and their citizens, even in instances when the effect of its use on citizens' evaluations and satisfaction does not yield tangible political activity and organization. Marc Lynch underscores the value of studying this more subtle and long-term domain of Internet effects: "A final area where state control might be fundamentally challenged is in its ability to control and dominate the public sphere. Here, longer-term shifts in individual competencies and in the broad information environment—rather than the more immediate 'tools' of political combat—matter most" (2011, 306).

This book also departs from the extant body of literature methodologically in two important ways. First, while the majority of the early studies focused on the Internet's effect in a single, developed or developing democracy,[2] this book opts for a comparative approach by considering the Internet's effect across a broad swath of countries. A comparative perspective favors a more nuanced approach by testing for effects that may be conditioned by social context. This is opposed to expecting the Internet's effect to be uniform across countries. Testing only for uniform effects across very different nations, with different governments, histories, and cultures, may cause researchers to fail to uncover meaningful effects that vary across borders. Additionally, comparative approaches will enable researchers to tease out and test the factors that condition those Internet effects, providing a more nuanced theoretical foundation for understanding the mechanisms that drive the Internet's political effects.

Second, this book takes a multi-method, multi-level approach—specifically, by marrying the large-N quantitative analysis of survey data at both the individual and country levels with randomized field experiments. This approach provides a strong empirical foundation for testing the nature of the Internet's influence by triangulating across data sources that complement one another's methodological strengths and weaknesses. If these tests reveal the same relationship between Internet use and democratic satisfaction at different levels of analysis, this will yield a more compelling set of results to illuminate the effects of the Internet than any single test could provide on its own.

Field experiments, specifically, offer many advantages to the study of political communication. First and foremost, they provide actual causal tests of the Internet's influence, filling a large and troubling gap in the extant literature. Additionally, field experiments complement the large-N quantitative analyses of survey data that tend to make up the bulk of Internet research, thus providing a more substantial empirical foundation for testing Internet effects. For example, while strong in external validity, large-N statistical analyses of survey data tend to be plagued with problems of weak internal validity. That is, survey instruments don't necessarily always measure what they purport to measure. These analyses also tend to suffer from weak causal inference. For example, can one be reasonably confident that it is Internet use that drives (dis)satisfaction? Or, is the reverse direction of causation more feasible?

On the other hand, experiments can be handicapped by weak external validity. That is, behavior in a laboratory doesn't always apply to the real world. But experiments allow the researcher to precisely control the variables of interest, thereby maximizing internal validity. Additionally, as a result of random assignment and careful control over the temporal ordering of variables, experiments provide the strongest test possible for causality. And by conducting randomized experiments in the field, it is also possible to increase external validity (at least relative to laboratory experiments) by having individuals use the Internet in a highly realistic setting. Thus, combining randomized field experiments with statistical analyses of survey data will provide the strongest possible empirical foundation for understanding the nature of the Internet's influence on evaluations and satisfaction.

Finally, as information and communication technologies continue to diffuse rapidly throughout the globe—often into regions that were previously nearly devoid of such capabilities—opportunities abound to explore how these technologies interact with and influence political attitudes, behaviors, and outcomes. Failing to get into the field to study firsthand how these new technologies are drastically and rapidly altering the communicative and informational landscapes in developing nations—and how those evolving landscapes then interact with the political realm—would mean missing out on the unique opportunities afforded by this particular period in time. It is my additional hope, therefore, that this book makes a case for the value of adding field experiments to the methodological toolbox belonging to Internet researchers.

Outline of the Book

In this chapter, I discussed how the Internet is meaningfully altering the contemporary information landscape and how this has important implications for the way people evaluate their governments. This is an essential component of studying the Internet's potential political effects, since not only does this alter the task of governance itself, but it is these evaluations that can and sometimes do encourage individuals to act and organize to effect political change. This chapter also provided two illustrations of the Internet's mirror-holding and window-opening functions, the primary mechanisms driving the Internet's influence on evaluations and satisfaction.

In chapter 2, I more fully introduce mirror-holding and window-opening. In doing so, I first situate the current Internet-led information revolution within the historical evolution of information landscapes. I then flesh out the assumptions of these mechanisms by grounding them in the relevant scholarly literature and illustrative anecdotes. This chapter concludes with a delineation of the specific hypotheses generated by these mechanisms as well as a roadmap of the specific tests of these hypotheses in the empirical chapters.

Chapter 3 then explores potential limitations of mirror-holding and window-opening. This entails a discussion of to what degree less formalized cyber-warfare tactics employed by governments discourage activism and critical discussion online; the degree to which state-sponsored propaganda and misinformation Internet campaigns can effectively drown out or distort independent content online; the potential restrictions imposed by the digital divide; whether mobile phones are really the technology that is having the most meaningful impact in developing countries; and whether there is actually "too much choice" between content online.

In the next chapters (4–7), I test the primary hypothesis undergirding this analysis by using several different methods that draw on distinct data sets at different levels of analysis. This multi-level, multi-method approach provides a rigorous and robust test of the Internet's effect on political evaluations by triangulating across methods that complement one another's strengths and weaknesses. Specifically, the primary hypothesis predicts that the Internet's effect on satisfaction is conditioned by the actual quality of democratic practices available in that country. This means that Internet use will increase satisfaction with democracy in nations boasting high-functioning democracies, but it will depress satisfaction in nations with weak democratic practices.

Through the randomized field experiments conducted in Bosnia and Herzegovina and Tanzania, I also test the Internet's influence on a broader range of relevant political evaluations. These include whether the Internet diminished citizens' trust in their government and national press, perceptions of the strength of democratic practices available, the terms through which individuals conceptualize democracy, support for the current political system in one's nation, and evaluations of the integrity of a controversial election.

In the concluding chapter (8), I discuss the implications of these findings and directions for future research. This chapter highlights specific sets of national factors that likely condition the effect of Internet use on evaluative processes, which can be primarily grouped into a nation's cultural, political, and economic characteristics. This discussion also considers factors that may predict when the Internet's effect on evaluations will trend in the prodemocratic direction and those which will encourage evaluations that may be contrary to democratization and democracy. The final section of this chapter considers the question of when and where these evaluations will be more likely to prompt political activity and organization offline, grounding this discussion in literature considering the form that citizenship and political organization will likely take in the digital age.

The findings uncovered in each of the analyses of survey data, as well as in the experiments, substantiate the Internet's clear, consistent, and considerable influence on democratic satisfaction and related evaluations. However, these results also reveal that one democratic gain, such as more critical evaluations of poorly performing governments, does not automatically set off a chain of entirely prodemocratic gains in citizens' attitudes and behaviors. Rather, the Internet's influence on evaluations, and subsequently on behavior, is a complex, contextually dependent process that in some instances will prove a double-edged sword for democracy and democratization.

CHAPTER 2

A Theory of Mirrors and Windows Online

To LAY OUT THE theoretical framework directing this research, I begin with a brief review of the history of information revolutions, which underscores just how profoundly the current Internet-led revolution is reshaping contemporary information landscapes. I then outline two mechanisms, mirror-holding and window-opening, that drive the Internet's influence on citizens' evaluations of their governments' performance.

In brief, mirror-holding contends that, by providing a broader and more extensive array of political information, the Internet holds up a mirror for users to better discern and reflect on how democratic practices (and governance more generally) actually function in their own country. Window-opening holds that the global nature of the Internet also opens a window for individuals to better view how governments function in other countries, particularly the advanced democracies that are most visible on the Internet. This provides users with a more realistic and globally consistent metric with which to make comparative evaluations about how well their own government functions.

I conclude by delineating four specific hypotheses generated by these mechanisms and a road map of the tests of these hypotheses in the following chapters. The primary hypothesis guiding this research predicts that exposure to the Internet will have a contingent effect on satisfaction with the quality of democratic practices available in one's own nation, so that Internet use will increase satisfaction in advanced democracies but depress satisfaction in nations with weak democratic practices. Delving more deeply into the effect of the Internet on related political evaluations, the second hypothesis posits that the Internet encourages individuals to reevaluate the quality of democratic practices available in their own nations in the same direction as their change in satisfaction. The third hypothesis, derived from window-opening, posits that Internet users will be more likely to conceptualize democracy in terms of the democratic rights and norms generally associated with advanced democracies. The final hypothesis pertains to the Internet's effect on evaluations of a specific democratic practice; namely, that Internet users will become more critical of the integrity of specific government processes—in this case, a controversial election—when they fail to meet established democratic standards.

A Historic Look at Information Revolutions: From Village Roads to Information Superhighways

A road is built to a village. Before the road, travel between the village and the nearest city required a circuitous two-hour drive through desolate mountainous terrain. With the road, this same passage can be traversed in a fraction of the time—less than twenty minutes by car. Or, if you'd rather, simply catch one of the reasonably priced buses that depart every hour.

With the road comes mobility. Along with the obvious physical mobility of persons comes mobility of resources, labor, goods, and information. Electricity and purified water soon follow the road into the village. Whereas nearly all the men of the village previously worked as farmers, barely producing enough to subsist, these men now commute to the city to work in factories for cash wages. Before the road was built, there was but one shop in the village—a ragtag, sparsely filled grocery store. The village now boasts seven well-stocked grocery stores and even a clothing shop selling jeans, cargo pants, and a small corner dedicated to Western men's suits and ties.

Perhaps more significant is the mobility of ideas, experience, and information that accompanies the road. Before the road came, few residents had ever left the village. The only news broadcast that reached them came through the village's sole radio, owned by the village chief and regarded by many as the "Devil's box." To most villagers, the idea of life outside the village's confines was nearly unfathomable—a world so unknown that to imagine such a thing was considered impious at best and downright dangerous at worst.

With the road comes the world. Over one hundred radio antennas now dot the village. Villagers and visitors flow in and out of the village, exchanging and circulating new ideas, experiences, and information. During visits to the city, the villagers sit in coffee shops, where they listen to radio programs bringing news from capitals across the world. They frequent movie houses where they are invited to step into another's shoes and visit an entirely new world.

This is the village of Balgat, Turkey, the scene of the opening parable in Daniel Lerner's classic work, *The Passing of Traditional Society* (1963). During his research, Lerner witnessed this remarkable transformation in a matter of four years, between 1950 and 1954. Roadways and transportation systems more generally are often identified as a primary catalyst for the globe's earliest information revolutions. Before the advent of electrical communication technology, information only moved as quickly as the persons who carried it, confined to the geographic spaces where those persons traveled. As water and roadway systems evolved and expanded, so did the mobility of persons and, as a consequence, the movement of ideas, experience, and information.

To fully appreciate the profundity of the current information revolution, it is useful to situate it within the historical context of the information revolutions that preceded it. Each of these revolutions had its roots in some fundamental shift in the system that determined how a population communicated its information.[1] These shifts derive from changes in one (or more) of the following three structural properties of communication systems: (1) how information is packaged, (2) how (and at what cost) that packaged information can be physically transmitted, and (3) the networks that determine who can send and receive those transmissions.

Beginning with the first type of shift, changes in the physical properties of how messages are encoded (i.e., how information can be packaged for communication) have been a powerful catalyst in the evolution of communication systems throughout history. From the spoken word to print, to picture, to video, to audio, to digital—how information is packaged determines not only the quality[2] and quantity of information that can be communicated but also the potential impact of that information.

The development of the written word, for example, meant that information could be archived. This made messages more permanent, thus increasing the quantity of information available for consumption and also enabling the information packaged in that message to abide well beyond the initial act of communication. Later, the ability to capture and package visual images for transmission further augmented the impact of communicated information, thanks to the very different properties of visual information relative to the written word. Visual images can communicate subconscious, emotional, and visceral information that cannot be as readily conveyed through words.

Turning to the second type of shift, it is advances in the mechanisms that transmit messages that spark an information revolution. Transmission technology determines how messages can be transported, to which geographic spaces, how quickly, and at what cost. The invention of the printing press in 1456, for example, gained significance with the development of postal systems that made the transmission of printed materials more regular and efficient. Perhaps the most significant development in transmission capability, as noted by Briggs and Burke in their comprehensive history of information and communication technology, *A Social History of Media: From Gutenberg to the Internet*, was the invention of the electric telegraph in 1837. It was not until this point that "the traditional link between transport and the communication of messages was broken" (2009, 20). The ability to transmit messages free of the constraint of having to physically carry them was monumental in terms of the capacity, speed, and geographic reach of a society's communication system. "Like canals, railways, and ocean highways, it linked the national and international markets, including stock exchanges and commodity markets. . . . It also speeded up the transmission of information, public and private, local, regional, national, and imperial, and this in the long run stood out as its most significant outcome. Distance was conquered" (134).

The third type of foundational shift in communication systems concerns the structure of the networks that determine who can send and who can receive which information. As history has proven time and again, this is a consequential component of communication systems: control over knowledge and information is a cornerstone of the distribution and balance of power in a society. The relationship shared by knowledge and power gained axiomatic status as long ago as 1597, thanks to Sir Francis Bacon's *Religious Meditations, of Heresies*. UN Secretary-General Kofi Annan famously reiterated this sentiment in his 1997 address at a World Bank conference, and its veracity was no less definitive four centuries later: "*Knowledge is power. Information* is liberating."

The penny press is one example of how changes in the audience that consumes specific types of information can have significant effects for a society. In the United States, where newspapers, at 6 cents apiece, had previously been unaffordable to the masses, the development of the penny press in the 1820s meant that a newspaper could now be purchased for a mere penny. Making newspapers affordable to the masses opened the door for important political developments. According to Bruce Bimber in *Information and American Democracy* (2003), the penny press, in conjunction with the establishment of the postal system, created the first nationwide audience for news. As a consequence, the idea of mass publics became feasible, leading to the nationalized political parties that are still an integral component of the U.S. political system today (albeit in a different form). The political effects of expanded newspaper readership were also evident during this same period in Europe, where newspapers are credited with constructing and concretizing the notion of "public opinion," or what Habermas (1991) describes as the "public sphere." This is illustrated in an 1844 book by two-time British Prime Minister Benjamin Disraeli, titled *Coningsby*, in which a character remarks, "God made man in His own image; but the Public is made by Newspapers" (qtd. in Briggs & Burke 2009, 187).

A more recent example is the development of wireless technology, pioneered by Guglielmo Marconi in the 1890s, which laid the technological groundwork for the development of radio and television in the following decades. These broadcast media made it possible to transmit information to geographic locations that were previously too remote or too unnavigable to reach. In developing countries, they have the added significance of circumventing the literacy requirement that constrains the audience for print media, opening up a whole new audience for the consumption of mediated information.

However, it is important not to overlook the other side of the equation set up by broadcast media. The significance of the network created by television and radio is not only which individuals it brings into its audience but also who is in the position to determine what information is sent to that audience. In the traditional broadcast system, messages emanate from a single point of origin out to an audience of many. This means that those who control transmission enjoy a powerful gatekeeping role in deciding which information is available for public consumption.

The most sinister examples of the consequences of this network structure are governments' use of broadcast media to spread state propaganda. Early standouts include Hitler and Stalin, who used the radio to actively prepare their populations to "support a war of aggression by firmly establishing in their minds a dichotomous, 'paranoid' world-picture" (White 1949, 173). This pernicious use of broadcast media by governments continues today. For example, the North Korean Chosun Central TV channel recently reported the results of a survey which confirmed that North Korea is the second "happiest" country in the world, beaten only by China. The other countries that round out the top five happiest list include Cuba, Iran, and Venezuela, in that order. Perhaps not so shockingly, South Korea ranked near the bottom at 152, while the United States came in dead last out of the 203 countries "surveyed" (*International Business Times* 2011).

Clearly, the actual demarcations between the origins of shifts in communication systems are fuzzy. Whether the point of origin of an information revolution is how messages are encoded, advances in the technology for transmitting messages, or changes in who is able to send and receive those messages, a shift in one is often accompanied (or at least followed quickly) by shifts in another. However, regardless of the origin, what unites each information revolution is its capacity to fundamentally remake a society's information landscape.

New media technologies are quickly, drastically, and simultaneously changing each of these three structural properties of contemporary communication systems. How we encode messages, the means for transmitting them, and the network that determines who can send and receive those messages has changed dramatically in the Internet age. The resulting advances in contemporary information landscapes are so profound that the term *revolution* is perhaps more appropriate now than ever before. As Clay Shirky writes in *Here Comes Everybody,* "We are living in the middle of the largest increase in expressive capability in the history of the human race. More people can communicate more things to more people than has ever been possible in the past, and the size and speed of this increase, from under one million participants to over one billion in a generation, makes the change unprecedented" (2008, 105–6).

This profound reshaping of contemporary information landscapes has direct and clear consequences for the range and quantity of information, as well as the set of criteria, that individuals draw upon to evaluate their governments. Specifically, I argue that the Internet's effect on these evaluations travels through two primary mechanisms: mirror-holding and window-opening. The following sections outline these functions and their assumptions in detail and embed them in the relevant scholarly literature.

Mirror-Holding

Even in developed democracies with robust press freedom, traditional media often fall well short of providing a fully accurate and comprehensive mirror for individuals to reflect on the performance of their government. This is a result of limitations stemming from both finite resources and the institutional features that determine the operation of traditional media outlets. In short, traditional media face budget, personnel, time, and space constraints, which combine to prevent the news from providing citizens with a complete picture of their nation's political workings. In addition, the traditional media's modi operandi—particularly those stemming from commercial, regulatory, and institutional imperatives—mean that the news media are not equally likely to report all stories and information.

Rather, since the traditional media must select a subset from the total body of possible stories, newsrooms tend to demonstrate preferences for reporting on specific topics through specific lenses (Entman 2003a; Entman 2003b; Graber 1997; Iyengar 1990; Iyengar 1994; Iyengar & Kinder 1987; Patterson 1994).This means that certain information, perspectives, and frames are either more or less likely than others to appear on the public stage. This is important because the subset of stories selected to appear on traditional media's public stage represent a mere fraction of the infinite stories that could be told in a given day. In Walter Lipmann's classic words, the press is "the beam of a searchlight that moves restlessly about, bringing one episode and then another out of darkness into vision" (1922, 229).

As such, even in developed democracies, the mirror that the traditional media provides to citizens with which to assess the performance of their government is limited in both scope and depth. In developing democracies, not only does this mirror tend to be even smaller and more one dimensional, but it can also often be somewhat clouded by the residue of historically contentious relationships between the press and government. Meanwhile, in undemocratic nations, the mirror afforded by traditional press better resembles the magical mirror of fairy tales—what is reflected is often not a reflection at all, but is instead a carefully controlled image projected onto the mirror by government officials so that every authoritarian government just happens to be the fairest of them all.

Censorship, poverty, individuals' inability to consume the Web in its entirety, and the presence of false information (each addressed in more detail later in this book) clearly prevent the Internet from providing citizens with a complete and perfect mirror image of their nation and government. It will, however, relay a reflection that is superior both in terms of size and depth to that which traditional media typically provide. Thus, the Internet improves the capacity of citizens in developed and developing democracies, and even in authoritarian nations, to make more informed and accurate evaluations of their governments, shaping their satisfaction accordingly.

This brings us to the first assumption undergirding the Internet's mirror-holding function:

Assumption 1: The Internet provides individuals with a greater volume of information than would otherwise be available through traditional media.

Scholars often attribute the Internet's capacity to relay a seemingly limitless array of information to the virtual absence of space and time constraints online, which increases the volume of available information as well as making it easier for individuals to access that information (Bimber 2001; Earl & Kimport 2011; Mossberger & Tolbert 2010; Scheufele & Nisbet 2002). One estimate regarding the amount of information that passes through the Internet on an average day places this number at "a staggering 40 petabytes, or 40×10^{15} bytes: a 4 followed by 16 zeros" (Cass 2007). As a point of reference, the entire amount of printed information housed by the Library of Congress is estimated at 10 terabytes (Lyman & Varian 2000), which amounts to only 1/4000th of the amount of information estimated to pass through the Internet on a typical day. And the quantity of information relayed through the Internet is expected to continue to mushroom. According to a recent study, annual global IP traffic will reach 966 exabytes (nearly 1 zettabyte) by 2015 (Cisco 2011).

Now compare the Internet's capacity to relay and archive information to that of traditional media. Newspapers are literally confined to reporting what the newspaper can physically carry in a given day. And the physical size of print newspapers is limited by logistical realities—most obviously, that newspapers must be physically transported to audiences and that legible font sizes can only be so small. Then consider broadcast television, which is restricted to presenting stories linearly, one at a time, for the allotted time that a news program airs. These constraints have been somewhat relaxed by cable television and the advent of the 24-hour news cycle; nevertheless, it is still the case that only one story can be told at a time per channel. Additionally, there tends to be a remarkable lack of diversity of stories covered during this 24-hour news cycle both within and across stations (Bockowski & de Santos 2007; Maier 2010). Thus, even after you add the running ticker tape of headlines to the amount of news a 24-hour news station tells in a given day, the amount is still dwarfed by the volume of information and stories that the Internet relays and archives on a daily basis.

Assumption 2: The Internet provides individuals with a more diverse range of information and perspectives than traditional media.

In addition to providing a greater volume of information, the content of the information on the Internet is distinct from and supports a broader range of perspectives than the traditional news media. This is most directly a result of the Internet's multipoint-to-multipoint configuration (Chadwick 2006; Mossberger, Tolbert, & McNeal 2008), which provides a convenient and accessible platform for the masses to contribute content—in the form of information, perspectives and opinions, anecdotes and personal experiences, memes, various creative works, and pictures and videos—to its informational landscape.

Contrast this with television and radio, which are configured as single-point-to-multipoint media in which information and content emanate from a single source out to the masses. This meant that during the broadcast era, the gatekeepers who determined which information made it past their posts exercised great control over determining the content of information available for public consumption. And since these gatekeepers often faced institutional and commercial constraints, specific stories from specific perspectives were either more or less likely to make it past their posts (Graber 1997), thus limiting the range of information and perspectives constituting traditional media landscapes.

The effect of the multipoint-to-multipoint configuration of the Internet on the diminished role of traditional media gatekeepers and the resulting increase in the range of perspectives and information available for public consumption is aptly summarized by Yochai Benkler: "The emergence of a networked public sphere is attenuating, or even solving, the most basic failings of the mass-mediated public sphere. . . . It provides an avenue for substantially more diverse and politically mobilized communication than was feasible in a commercial mass media with a small number of speakers and a vast number of passive recipients. The views of many more individuals and communities can be heard" (2006, 465).

While online news consumers in developed democracies still tend to overwhelmingly frequent the websites associated with traditional news media outlets (Hindman 2009), this does not mean they are exposed to the same *content* that they would be in a world without the Internet. This is evidenced by a study that compared the content of the print and online versions of the *New York Times,* which revealed that online news sites belonging to traditional media outfits provide individuals with different news stories than their own print versions (Althaus & Tewksbury 2002). In another study, Maier (2010) finds that although there is a considerable degree of overlap between online and offline platforms belonging to news outlets in terms of the topics covered, "major Web news sites today do not simply mirror the selection of news stories leading in print and broadcast . . . audiences turning to news Web sites will find the dominant stories of the day, as well as a selection of news reports offering fresh perspective on events shaping the nation and the world. It is also noteworthy that online news media offered greater news breadth than any other media sector" (557).

Also consider that newsrooms do not have sufficient resources to station journalists and cameras in all places at all times. This means that the decision of where to station those resources largely determines which stories newsrooms can tell. Compare this to the Internet age, in which average citizens can contribute eyewitness accounts, information, and pictures and video footage to the public stage, dramatically expanding the range of perspectives and information available for public consumption. For example, during the Egyptian revolution, Tufekci and Wilson (2012) found that nearly half of the surveyed individuals who had participated in the protests used multimedia to disseminate eyewitness pictures and videos from the protest. And in the Syrian conflict, it was pictures and videos taken by civilians on camera phones and then distributed online that provided some of the first documentation of the use of chemical weapons in an attack of a Damascus suburb—catapulting the conflict to the center of global dialogue (D. Bennett 2013).

The capacity for user-generated content to shift the public dialogue is further highlighted by the many instances in which stories that first broke on the Internet gathered enough steam that they eventually compelled the traditional media to also cover them—stories that likely would not have been told at all in a pre-Internet era. Perhaps one of the most famous cases in the United States is the Drudge Report's role in breaking the Monica Lewinsky scandal, leading to the impeachment of President Bill Clinton. More recent examples in the United States include a video of a six-year-old girl being patted down by airport security, which was posted online by her parents. After this video (and similar videos of other children) circulated widely on YouTube, mainstream media picked up the story. The resulting public stir ultimately prompted the TSA to loosen its search guidelines for children (CBS News 2011). In another story, a group of American troops returning from war created a video complaining about the exorbitant baggage fees they had to pay to Delta Air Lines, which amounted to over $2,800. Once again, this story picked up steam online, drawing the attention of mainstream media and resulting in Delta's changing its baggage fees policy for military personnel (Pawlowski 2011).

Additionally, several studies confirm that the Internet empowers citizens to seek out information and perspectives from nontraditional sources (Dahlgren 2005; Horrigan 2006; Horrigan et al. 2004; Tewksbury & Althaus 2000). Citizens in the United States, for example, report using the Internet for news because they are dissatisfied with news provided by the traditional media (Tolbert & McNeal 2003), suggesting that users believe that the Internet provides them with information or perspectives not available through traditional media. Accordingly, a 2004 Pew/Internet report found that 24 percent of Net users report visiting "alternative" news sites, including international news organization websites. The same study also found that online news consumers are actually more likely to be exposed to information from competing sources—such as opposing candidates, parties, and issue groups—than those who gather news from traditional outlets (Horrigan et al. 2004).

The Internet's capacity to increase the range of information available for public consumption is also evident even in countries with the most successful Internet censorship policies. Citing a number of earlier studies, Earl and Kimport (2011) highlight the Internet's capacity to spread messages that circumvent mainstream media even in "hostile climates" and in ways that are "more difficult for governments to block" (25). Accordingly, examples abound of users evading sophisticated Internet regulatory systems to disseminate political information that would otherwise remain suppressed.

This is the case even in China, the nation with arguably the most sophisticated regulatory system, which combines the Great Firewall that actively blocks "sensitive" content from entering the country, the less overt approach of deliberately manipulating search engine results, and a large human force that actively monitors and then shames and punishes Internet users who do not conform to established guidelines for proper use (Conaway 2013). Despite all of this, however, "the Internet in China often disseminates forbidden information and opinions through e-mail, instant messaging, blogs, and bulletin board forums or through political expressions disguised as non-political comments" (Lum 2006, 2).

The potential for the Internet's multipoint-to-multipoint configuration to broaden the range of voices and perspectives available in countries with sophisticated censorship systems is particularly well illustrated by China's microblog website, Sina Weibo. This website serves as the nation's alternative to Twitter, which is officially blocked in China. Since its launch in 2009, Sina Weibo has grown exponentially, with nearly 400 million users by the end of 2012 (Rigg 2012). This means that more than half of all Internet users in China had microblog accounts as of 2012.

Not surprisingly, Weibo is actively censored by the government (Sullivan 2012), using as their primary method employing thousands of individuals who actively monitor the website for content deemed controversial or in violation of censorship regulations, which is then deleted. Despite this, Weibo still serves as a platform for citizens to discuss controversial issues and criticize the Chinese government. According to Carnegie Mellon researchers, while there is clear evidence of censorship via deleted posts that referred to controversial political and social topics—such as Falun Gong, specific political activists, and pornography—the deletion of this content is inconsistent and incomplete: "While most of these terms are officially blocked on Sina's search interface, very few of them are deleted with 100 percent coverage" (Bamman, O'Connor, & Smith 2012). In further support of this, an extensive analysis by King, Pan, and Roberts (2013) of millions of social media posts to 1,400 distinct social media websites in China reveals that government censors are actually relatively permissive toward critical and even vitriolic discussion of the government by citizens, but they draw the line when this discussion starts to suggest some sort of offline activity or organization.

Often political information online in nations where the Internet is censored is disguised as nonpolitical communication; one of the more popular forms that this takes is that of humor. In the case of Egypt, in the months leading up to the protests, Egyptians used Twitter to exchange jokes regarding President Mubarak such as: "What is the perfect day for Hosni Mubarak? A day when nothing happens" (Lynch, Glasser, & Hounshell 2011). Others created satirical Facebook pages mocking prominent Egyptian leaders. Additionally, "widely circulated video mash-ups depict Mubarak and his entourage as the characters of a mafia movie or unlikely action heroes, including one spoofing a Star Wars poster with Mubarak standing in for the evil Emperor Palpatine" (Amrani 2011).

Political discussion online can also be explicit and overt in these countries, however. As of 2011, Arabic ranked as the seventh-most-spoken language on the Internet. There are an estimated 70,000 to 100,000 active blogs operating from within Iran, and despite its authoritarian government, much of the Iranian blogosphere is colored by a decidedly critical tone of dissent, with writing styles described as "witty, subversive, and ingenious" (Naughton 2006). Moreover, "activists have used their blogs to organize demonstrations and boycotts, and to criticize corruption and government policies" (Ambah 2006).

In Cuba, individuals buy or rent passwords and codes from the small number of individuals and companies cleared by the government for Internet access. And it is clear that some of these individuals use their Internet access to disseminate political information and promote critical discussion online. The potential impact of this has not been lost on the Cuban government: "U.S. diplomatic cables published by WikiLeaks in December 2010 revealed that the Cuban regime is more afraid of bloggers than of 'traditional' dissidents" (Reporters Without Borders 2011).

Another potent channel for successful circumvention of government regulation is the cyber connection shared by expatriates and activists remaining in the homeland, enabling the international exchange of subversive information and coordination of protest activities. One example is The Other Russia organization, headed by former Russian chess champion Garry Kasparov, who uses the Internet to organize and exchange information with dissenters still living in Russia, as well as to publish videos of police brutality against protest rallies on YouTube (Kasparov 2007). According to the website, "theotherrussia.org is an independent news and opinion website dedicated to presenting information from and about the political situation in Russia. Our emphasis is on news that is supressed [*sic*] or distorted by media sources in Russia, which are controlled directly or indirectly by the Kremlin" (Greengard 2011).

The reform-minded, expatriate-run Eritrean website Dehai offers another example of a diasporic community that set up websites to facilitate access to critical information for audiences remaining in the home country. While the majority of visitors are Eritreans abroad, approximately 20 percent of daily visits originate from within the country of Eritrea itself: "Eritreans abroad use the Internet as a transnational public sphere where they produce and debate narratives of history, culture, democracy and identity. Through the Web the diaspora has mobilized demonstrators, amassed funds for war, debated the formulation of the constitution, and influenced the government of Eritrea" (Bernal 2006).

In another example, Nigerian journalist Omoyele Sowore was the "first to publish a photo of the Nigeria-born 'underwear bomber' arrested in December 2009, and when a suicide bombing . . . shook a United Nations building in Abuja, Nigeria's capital, he was the first to publish on-the-ground reports and photos" (Speigel 2011). In April of 2011, his coverage of the Nigerian presidential election attracted over 8 million page views in a single month. However, Sowore is not stationed in Nigeria. Armed with a laptop, Sowore publishes his reports from his office located more than five thousand miles away in Manhattan. Working from afar enables Sowore to distribute information regarding corruption and government malfeasance with impunity—the very sort of information that would likely invite severe repercussions from the Nigerian government if he were reporting as a member of the domestic press.

In fact, the City University of New York has created the International Reporting Program, a graduate program dedicated to training expatriate journalists in order to bolster this sort of "in absentia press reporting" (Speigel 2011). The program provides training in language, digital technology, and entrepreneurial journalism. Recent students of this program have already built sizeable followings. The *Lanka Standard,* created by a Sri Lankan student of this program, attracted more than 65,000 visitors within three months of its launch, with many visitors accessing the website from within Sri Lanka. Another website, *Iran dar Jahan,* created by an Iranian graduate of this program, registers 70,000 visitors a month (Speigel 2011).

The struggle between governments bent on Internet censorship and citizens committed to circumventing that censorship is often also joined by third parties, including foreign governments and international organizations who lend their weight to the side of Internet freedom. For example, the U.S. government provides counter-censorship software to Chinese Internet users (Lau 2005; Lum 2006). Moreover, in 2011, the U.S. State Department offered grants between $500,000 and $8 million (for a total of $30 million) to support development of counter-censorship software as well as "technologies, techniques, and training to enhance the security of mobile communications" to prepare and protect foreign activists (qtd. in Williams 2011).

International organizations and NGOs represent another third-party effort to liberate Internet use in countries with strict Internet regulation. The most prominent example is the controversial nonprofit organization known as WikiLeaks, whose self-described objective is the development of "an uncensorable Wikipedia for untraceable mass document leaking and analysis. Our primary interests are oppressive regimes in Asia, the former Soviet bloc, Sub-Saharan Africa and the Middle East, but we also expect to be of assistance to those in the west who wish to reveal unethical behavior in their own governments and corporations. We aim for maximum political impact; this means our interface is identical to Wikipedia and usable by non-technical people" (http://wikileaks.org/).

Finally, as in developed countries, the Internet also broadens the range of information that is available for public consumption offline through more formal channels and traditional media. Here too, anecdotes demonstrate the capacity for Internet-born stories to eventually force the recognition of the traditional media and even government officials. For example, in China, in order to compete with the Internet, traditional state-run media have shown a greater propensity to report stories that would have remained out-of-bounds in the pre-Internet era: "As Chinese citizens increasingly use the Internet to get news, share videos, vent frustrations and expose abuses of power, leaders are being forced to react publicly to their concerns. Government officials are also adapting traditional media-control techniques to the information age—including sending out press releases and approved articles on topics that once would have been completely suppressed" (Lawrence 2008).

For example, consider the now-popular phrase among Chinese netizens, "My father is Li Gang." This phrase, now commonly spoken ironically to connote the avoidance of responsibility and being above the law, was inspired by a 2010 drunk-driving incident in which the son of the deputy director of Baoding Public Security Bureau struck two university students, killing one and injuring the second. After he failed to stop at the scene of the accident, campus security and angry bystanders intercepted the driver, Li Qiming, who bragged, "Go ahead, sue me if you dare, my father is Li Gang" (qtd. in Diamond & Plattner 2012, 70).

When it was clear that the school and government officials were planning to sweep the incident under the rug, incensed students and protesters organized a large-scale human flesh search engine (i.e., a massive human collaboration aided by the use of social media technology and the Internet to identify individuals engaged in untoward behavior). These netizens uncovered information about Li Gang and Li Qiming and created a sustained online campaign to call attention to this injustice, including posting pictures of Li Qiming, creating a satirical music video, revealing that he had plagiarized a large portion of his thesis, and inserting the phrase "My father is Li Gang" into traditional Chinese poetry and prose (Know Your Meme 2011; Global Voices 2010):

> The luminous moonshine before my bed,
> Is thought to be the frost fallen on the ground.
> I lift my head to yell at the security gard [sic],
> My father is Li Gang.

Despite initially preferring to ignore the protesters, including releasing an official statement to Chinese media outlets instructing them not to report on this story (which was subsequently leaked online), the story continued to gain traction both online and offline (China Digital Times 2010). Ultimately, this forced the government to prosecute Li Qiming. Over a year after committing the crime, he was sentenced to six years in prison and ordered to pay a large sum of money to the victims' families (Barboza 2011).

In another example, consider the months leading up to the 2006 election in Singapore, during which an audio clip satirizing the Singaporean government was downloaded 110,000 times, with the number of individuals possibly exposed to that clip considerably larger. Acknowledging the power and popularity of this clip, Member of Parliament Baey Yam Keng called on the government to "relax rules on traditional media so people can engage openly in meaningful and level-headed discussions about the Government and Singapore politics. . . . This will allow the Government to address and rebut criticism—something it cannot do if the criticism 'goes underground' and appears only on the Internet" (Low 2006).

The effect of the Internet in the 2006 election was evident in the 2011 campaign season, when it prompted the government to make concrete changes in Singapore's campaign laws regarding online messaging. "This tightly controlled city-state has taken a step into the unknown in advance of its parliamentary elections on Saturday, loosening its grip on political discourse in the unruly world of the Internet" (Mydans 2011). Prominent blogger Alex Au points to the effect that the Internet has also had offline: "Online coverage has pushed the main pro-government newspaper, *The Straits Times*, to publish fuller and not always critical news and photographs of opposition campaigns" (qtd. in Mydans 2011).

Finally, the Internet also better empowers individuals to transcend intranational boundaries to share information that would otherwise likely remain muffled. For instance, women constitute a sizeable percentage of Saudi Arabia's blogosphere. As Ambah (2006) observes, "Young women make up half the bloggers in the kingdom. . . . lured by the possible anonymity of the medium, Saudi women have produced a string of blogs filled with feminist poetry, steamy romantic episodes and rants against their restricted lives and patriarchal society." For example, in 2013 Saudi Arabian women created an online petition in support of their planned October 26th protest against the country's long-standing ban against women driving (http://oct 26driving.com/), which amassed nearly 11,000 signatures over the course of just four days before the webpage was blocked in the nation (Jamjoom 2013a, 2013b). The movement gained international attention when a cleric warned that driving threatens women's reproductive health by damaging their ovaries, prompting Saudi Arabian women to take to the Internet again to respond to, and often mock, the cleric's claims under the Twitter hashtag: #WomensDrivingAffectsOvariesAndPelvises. Two such Tweets include: "What a mentality we have. People went to space and you still ban women from driving. Idiots," and "Please respect ourminds [*sic*] If u don't want us to drive at least come up with good reasonable excuse" (Chappell 2013).

Clearly, despite Internet censorship, more political information from more perspectives is now available for consumption in these countries than would be available in a world without the Internet. This is because censorship of the Internet is simply less successful and efficient for governments than censorship of traditional media. As Andrew Chadwick explains, "regulating television is actually pretty straightforward in comparison with the

Internet" (2006, 7), which he attributes to the fundamental differences that distinguish the Internet from traditional broadcast media. These include its being a multipoint-to-multipoint medium as opposed to television's single-point-to-multipoint configuration; its being primarily global in orientation, whereas television is more nationally oriented; its drastically lower entry costs of content production; and the existence of well-known technical fixes to state censorship available to Internet users, which include "proxy servers, encryption, and other anonymity tools to route around controls" (7).

In light of this, it is worthwhile to consider whether the effect of mirror-holding on satisfaction and evaluations is the most pronounced in these fledgling pseudo-democratic and nondemocratic states, in which states previously enjoyed a high level of control over traditional broadcast media. While Internet users in countries with censored Internet may have substantially less access to information about their own nations and governments compared to individuals living in countries with unregulated Internet, the Internet nevertheless makes decidedly more information accessible to these citizens than would be the case otherwise. And, in these information-scarce nations, even a marginal increase in access to information can have great significance. Moreover, since these individuals are living in nations with weak or nonexistent democratic practices, the information that does slip through the cracks will be substantially more likely to reflect poorly rather than positively on the government.

In sum, the Internet provides a broader and more critical range of information for public consumption—in democratic, democratizing, as well as nondemocratic countries—than would be available in the world of traditional media. This enables the Internet to hold up a more nuanced and accurate mirror for citizens to better reflect on the actual performance of their governments, with important implications for the evaluations and satisfaction that citizens derive from that information.

Assumption 3: Individuals are exposed to political information about their own government online.

With few exceptions (Scheufele & Nisbet 2002; Tewksbury & Althaus 2000), research shows that Internet exposure increases users' levels of political knowledge (Davis 1999; Johnson & Kaye 2003; Kenski & Stroud 2006; Mossberger, Tolbert, & McNeal 2008; Xenos & Moy 2007). For example, in a study of 14- to 22-year-old users, Pasek (2006) demonstrated that the Internet's positive effect on political awareness exceeded that of any other mass medium, including newspapers. As to whether individuals incorporate Internet-acquired information into political evaluations, respondents in a 2004 study reported integrating election information obtained online into their ultimate vote choices (Farnsworth & Owen 2004).

Moreover, all of these studies were conducted in information-abundant countries. The fact that political knowledge increased, even marginally, in countries where populations are already relatively saturated with political information is meaningful. An even larger implication of this finding is the Internet's capacity to increase political knowledge in nations where citizens have traditionally been largely deprived of such information, suggesting the effect could be considerably larger in these countries.

Skeptics, on the other hand, have worried that the vast quantity of information on the Internet may actually inhibit information acquisition by overwhelming Internet users. However, research has shown that appropriate organization and screening practices can be developed to minimize the effects of data glut (Hiltz & Turoff 1985; Nielson 1995). In addition, Benkler notes the rise of "non-market, peer-produced alternative sources of filtration and accreditation" that serve as mechanisms to filter, focus attention around, and then validate claims and their sources through informal peer review (2006, 12).

Additionally, it is important to differentiate exposure to information that may shape subsequent political evaluations and the capacity to retain and recall that information. It may be unlikely that Internet users will be able to effectively retain the information they acquire about their government and recall that information upon command. However, the "online" model of information processing (Hastie & Park 1986) suggests that processing information from the Internet need not be such a costly endeavor. Rather, the online model describes opinion formation as a product of calling to mind a running tally, which is conceived as "a counter in working memory that integrates new information into a 'running tally' of one's current impression" (Lodge et al. 1989, 401). This suggests that individuals can efficiently integrate new information and update their opinions without having to store each piece of information in their permanent memory.

Finally, while information acquisition is often the result of deliberate, purposive effort, it is worth noting that users can also acquire information as a byproduct of using the Internet for other purposes (Tewksbury et al. 2001). In Mossberger and Tolbert's words, "*online news may accidentally mobilize individuals* who are online for other reasons" (2010, 205, emphasis in original). While one-third of the American population reported using the Internet to get news on a typical day in 2010—a number that spikes to 44 percent when mobile phones, social networks, and podcasts are included

(Pew Research Center 2010)—a report by the Pew Research Center (2004) shows that consumers encounter news on the Internet via non-deliberate exposure as well. This report found that 73 percent of Internet users "bumped into news" after going online for another purpose.

Underscoring the import of this sort of incidental exposure, Tewksbury, Weaver, and Maddex (2001) found that incidental exposure to news increased individuals' awareness of current affairs. Recent research by Lee (2009) further substantiates incidental exposure to news online, revealing that Internet users were particularly likely to run into political information online when seeking entertainment or sports news. Thus, classic studies of traditional media, which confirmed the tendency for political information to piggyback on entertainment-oriented use of media (Baum 2003), appear to also apply to the Internet.[3]

Consider, for example, the incidental exposure to political information that piggybacks on social media use such as Facebook. Most Facebook users log on to follow their friends and to contribute their own status updates and pictures for their friends to follow them. However, people also share links to news stories that interest them, which frequently show up on their friends' news feeds with short captions and pictures. Thus, users need not even click on these links to be incidentally exposed to the information that these news stories carry. Moreover, it is also the case that people do click on these links and sometimes even share them with their own friends by re-posting them to their own profile pages.

A recent Pew study found that 80 percent of Internet users receive or send links to news stories through email. More generally, they find that "people's experience of news, especially on the Internet, is becoming a shared social experience as people swap links in emails, post news stories on their social networking feeds, highlight news stories in the Tweets, and haggle over the meaning of events in discussion threads" (Purcell et al. 2010, 2). This means that individuals not originally seeking political information are nevertheless exposed to it as a byproduct of using the Internet to socialize with and keep informed about their friends.

The field experiment in Tanzania (presented in chapter 7) provides further support for the intentional use of the Internet to gather political information as well as the tendency for political information to piggyback on nonpolitical Internet use. Beginning with deliberate political information acquisition, the results revealed that 95 percent of the participants created an email address, 64 percent reported that they created a Facebook account, and 64 percent reported reading blogs while online. Meanwhile, 61 percent of participants reported that they "mostly" used the media to look for information and news, 32 percent reported that they "mostly" used the Internet for social media (e.g., Facebook, Twitter, Myspace), and only 13 percent stated that they "mostly" used the Internet for entertainment (e.g., watch videos on YouTube, listen to music). Finally, more than one-third of the participants stated that they specifically followed information about the 2010 Tanzanian election on the Internet either regularly or sometimes. Clearly, using the Internet to seek out political information was a priority to these individuals.

As for inadvertent exposure to political content online, in an Internet café in Tanzania I watched a woman clad in a full burqa click through more than ninety pages of a website showing Western women's apparel—page after page after page, for over an hour. It's not difficult to imagine that this woman was inadvertently exposed to more information than simply how women in Western democracies dressed differently.

Window-Opening

Airplanes, films, telephones, and traditional broadcast media represent only a few channels that have long opened windows that enable individuals to peer into the daily lives of those living in other nations. Voice of America, for example, began transmitting daily radio broadcasts of American current events, news, and popular culture into European, Asian, and African nations in 1942 in an effort to export American values and counter Nazi and Soviet propaganda (Whitton 1951). Thus, although the current phase of globalization is not unique in transcending national borders, thanks to the Internet, the speed and breadth with which information and communication can be relayed worldwide is unprecedented. Voice of America itself has embraced the Internet to extend its reach and expand its programming, which, according to current estimates, reaches 134 million audience members speaking more than forty different languages worldwide (Broadcasting Board of Governors 2013).

Additionally, information originating from or pertaining to foreign countries traditionally tended to be filtered through some combination of media gatekeepers (guided by commercial and institutional imperatives) and government officials (guided by domestic and foreign policy interests). In contrast, the Internet facilitates the international exchange of information relatively less subject to the oversight of traditional monitors. Therefore, while individuals have long been able to observe the lives of those in other nations, the windows afforded by traditional media tended to be relatively small, fleeting, and often obscured or screened by official powers.

The Internet, on the other hand, opens potentially panoramic windows through which to better view how democracy and governance more generally function in other nations, affording average citizens vantage points that are more accessible and less obstructed by elites and government officials. As Chadwick (2006) explains, "While a computer connected to the Net grants you potential (if not actual) access to all parts of a global network, owning a television does not." He attributes this to the national gatekeepers who determine which content from foreign countries will air on the domestic television networks, whereas the international content accessible via the Internet is markedly less subject to the oversight of these national monitors. This means that the Internet differs from traditional broadcast media due to its "potentially global user base," which ensures its status as the "largest *global* medium, by a long way" (2006, 11).

This global orientation of the Internet further influences citizens' satisfaction with their own governments by providing more globally consistent metrics with which to evaluate them. Essentially, in addition to providing more robust information about one's own government, the Internet also alters their expectations and criteria by opening a window that exposes individuals to more information about how governments function in other countries, shaping their satisfaction accordingly. This is aided by the fact that "new information and communication . . . undermine the ability of ruling elites to manage what civil society learns about political cultures in other countries" (Howard 2010, 149). And thanks to the structure of the Internet, users are particularly likely to be exposed to information about advanced democracies, thereby encouraging individuals to adopt a more globally consistent conception of governance dominated by the norms commonly associated with advanced democracies.

The significance of this more globally consistent metric is illustrated by *congruence theory*, which posits that satisfaction with democracy is contingent on individuals' beliefs about what actually constitutes democracy (Anderson & Guillory 1997; Kornberg & Clarke 1994; Miller et al. 1997). The capacity to define democracy, therefore, is a crucial component in shaping support for democratic governments, particularly those in transition. Thus, exposure to information about how democracy functions in the advanced democracies that dominate the Internet will restrict a government's latitude in defining the terms through which its own citizens conceptualize and evaluate their own country's democratic practices.[4]

The Internet's capacity to promote a more globally consistent conception of what constitutes good democratic governance becomes particularly powerful in light of the tendency for leaders of authoritarian and sub-par democratic countries to glorify and propagandize their responsiveness and democratic virtues to their own citizens, despite the international community's awareness of the democratic failings of many of these countries. Take the Chinese government's self-congratulation on its official website, which proclaims that it has made great gains in "incorporating respecting and safeguarding human rights with strengthening democracy." It is this very disjuncture between how a government defines its own "democratic" performance and how that same government's (un)democratic character is revealed online that is central to the Internet's effect on citizens' evaluations of their governments.

Finally, beyond advanced democracies, consider also the Internet's capacity to expose individuals to more information about how other governments function in democratizing and authoritarian countries. This vantage point provides individuals with a broader view of a larger set of nations, which lends itself to identifying patterns that are consistent across government type (Diamond 2008). This will plausibly provide an even broader range of globally consistent metrics, which will further inform the expectations and set of criteria that individuals employ in evaluating their own governments. For example, consider whether in the case of the Arab Spring exposure to information online regarding the shared failures of authoritarian governments in this region may have further influenced the information and criteria that shaped individuals' evaluations of their own governments.

Each of the three aforementioned assumptions also underlies window-opening. However, window-opening requires two additional assumptions:

Assumption 4: Compared to traditional media, the Internet exposes individuals to more information about how governments function in other countries.

The relative speed and ease with which the Internet transports information across large geographic spaces and national borders makes more information available for public consumption about foreign nations, in greater volume and with greater diversity, than was previously possible through the traditional media system. This relative lack of geographic constraints facilitates "the dissemination of information at volumes, in speeds, and with spatial coverage never before witnessed. . . . By letting information in, connectivity exposes information of an external origin to a domestic audience. By getting information out, connectivity internationalizes previously domestic information" (Richards 2002, 161–62). In support of this, a 2006 study found that the Internet contributed to gains in international knowledge, particularly among younger users, as a result of connecting "individuals to the international community by helping them increase their knowledge of the world, facilitating their sense of belonging to the greater world, and motivating them to participate in international events and foreign volunteer opportunities" (Kwak et al. 2006, 206–7).

A formal channel through which information travels between countries is international news websites. For example, 18 percent of Americans who consume news online visit the website of an international news organization during a typical day (Purcell et al. 2010). BBC Online is available in twenty-seven languages, ranging from Arabic to Burmese, to Portuguese, to Swahili, to Ukrainian. In March of 2010 the BBC reported that its news site attracted 7.3 million visitors weekly from across the globe. Moreover, although many American cable companies still refuse to carry the Al Jazeera English news channel, this did not preclude Americans from searching out news from this organization online. During the early weeks of the Egyptian protests, the *New York Times* reported that traffic to Al Jazeera's English-language website had increased by 2,500 percent, that its live stream had been viewed over 4 million times, and that 1.6 million of those views had come from the United States (Stelter 2011).

It is clear that the "Internet has reduced the impact of distance, making foreign media easily available" (Mossberger & Tolbert 2010, 206). However, there is also evidence of political information exchanged transnationally through less formal channels on the Internet. For example, consider the website www.sorryeverybody.com. This website began after the reelection of George W. Bush in 2004, motivated by the desire of one college student to communicate to the world that not all Americans were in favor of what their government was doing. James Zetlen, a 20-year-old student at the University of Southern California, posted a picture of himself holding a sign stating, "Sorry World. (We tried.) –Half of America."

Then, over the coming weeks and months, Americans across the country contributed their own apologies, resulting in an archive of thousands of such photos. Various signs include: "World—I deeply apologize to any countries that have been or will be hurt under Bush's control. We're very sorry. Love—56% of Illinois"; "I am so sorry for the loss of life this election will bring with it"; "We are really sorry. Love, the non-millionaires of America"; "Sorry, World! Bush somehow convinced us that war was peace, slavery was freedom and tax cuts for the rich somehow benefited us! When will we learn?" (See figure 2.1 for more examples of these posts.)

Within weeks, the website had more than a 27 million hits (BBC 2004). The messages on this website reached their intended audience: many of the millions of visitors to this website were individuals living in foreign nations who started submitting their own pictures accepting the apologies and con-

FIGURE 2.1 Photo Gallery Samples from www.SorryEverybody.com

tributing their own views. This eventually spawned the response site, www
.apologiesaccepted.com. A smattering of these responses include: "Thank
you from Palestine to the amazing 49%. We will never let the dream of
peace and a homeland die. Awaiting 2008"; "Turkey loves 49% and those
who r against war. Stop killing babies and civilians in Felluce Mr. Bush.
Shame on you 51%"; "Been there, done that. I forgive 100% of you. –The
Philippines"; "Thank you for trying. Hope you all to be happy. Wish peace!
From China"; "Greece Accepts. Greece Stands with you. We gave you phi-
losophy, democracy, Olympics, and love. Use 'em, please." (See figure 2.2 for
additional examples of posts.)

Clearly, a fair amount of political information is communicated through
this website between citizens living across the globe, both directly and indirectly. Most obviously, Americans publicly linked themselves (and their images) to a site that is overtly challenging the incumbent government, demonstrating a lack of fear of government reprisal. This site also documents the
vigor of political debate in the United States and that not all citizens were
monolithically in support of President Bush, a rather unpopular figure in
many nations. The responses from individuals living in other countries also

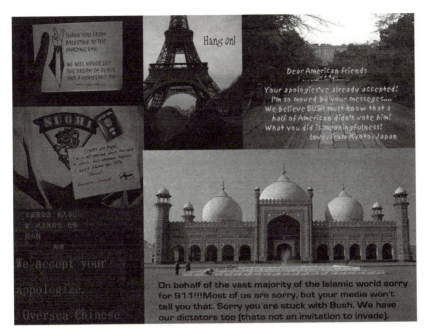

FIGURE 2.2 Photo Gallery Samples from www.ApologiesAccepted.com

revealed information about their own countries and governments as well as their attitudes toward the U.S. government and its people.

Beyond specific websites and formal organization online, the Internet also augments both the affordability and the accessibility of cross-border communication through online phone connections (e.g., Skype), instant messaging, social networking, and blogging. This facilitates more frequent communication between expatriates and their friends and family back home. In 2009, free Skype-to-Skype international calls amounted to 54 billion minutes (Wauters 2010). Thus, individuals who have immigrated to other countries can relate their personal experiences and observations more easily and frequently to those still living in their homeland.

In sum, the Internet facilitates and expedites the international exchange of information. Some of this is through formal channels, while other communication is through informal channels. Some takes place between people who already know each other, while other travels through networks of individuals that are only connected through the Internet—such as through blogs, various social networks (e.g., Twitter, Facebook), and membership in various international organizations. Finally, some of this information travels through deliberate uses of the Internet to gather political information, while other information piggybacks onto nonpolitical uses of the Internet. All in all, more information is exchanged transnationally over the Internet, often outside of the jurisdiction of traditional gatekeepers and government officials, at a greater speed and capacity than has ever before been possible.

Assumption 5: Internet users are particularly likely to be exposed to information pertaining to advanced democracies.

The Internet's first significant application was in the United States, and it diffused first to other highly developed democracies (Curtis 2011). As a result, the majority of the most popular websites across the globe originated in these countries. Essentially, individuals and groups in developed democracies constructed the vast majority of the Internet's original informational landscape—the same websites that now constitute the Internet's "large, strongly connected core" (Kleinberg & Lawrence 2001, 1849). In the language of social network analysis, thanks to the "rich-get-richer" phenomenon, in which the connectedness or popularity of web pages is said to take the form of a highly skewed power law distribution, a small number of pages tend to boast very high levels of connectedness (Kleinberg & Lawrence 2001).

This is because the likelihood that a website will acquire a link from a new website is a function of how many other websites that original website is already connected to. Websites have an incentive to connect to other websites that are already highly connected, since this brings more immediate benefits in terms of enhancing one's own website's connectedness. As a consequence, Internet users are particularly likely to be exposed to these highly connected websites, which were primarily created in developed democracies and now constitute the Internet's core. Evidence of this pro–advanced democracy bias in popular websites abounds. For instance, as of 2013, twenty-nine of the forty most popular web pages worldwide are based in a developed democracy or are a nation-specific offshoot of a website that originated in a developed democracy, such as Google India (Alexa 2013).

In fact, individuals need not search out details specifically pertaining to the practices of advanced democracies to be exposed to information that may cause them to update their own conceptions of democracy. Stories about elections, protests, demonstrations, and political scandals are obvious topics that convey information about how democracy functions in other countries. Even information about more mundane day-to-day topics and activities (such as the presence of women in the workplace, celebrity lifestyles, popular culture, and high-profile criminal cases) or simply downloading the latest season of a popular U.S. or U.K. television series can illuminate how democratic practices function in advanced democracies. Moreover, entertainment produced in developed democracies is ubiquitous online, even in countries with extensive Internet censorship. Sydell (2008) writes that "although the Chinese government does a good job of censoring political content online, it's been more lax about cultural matters. More than 200 million Chinese now have access to American TV online, for example. Downloading has become so popular that it's even cutting into the profits of vendors who sell pirated DVDs." A 2005 UNESCO report identifies the Internet as a central force in the recent expansion of the international trade of cultural products. Thus, various nonpolitical cultural goods and information transmitted online can effectively communicate how advanced democracies function, further encouraging Internet users to acquire a more globally consistent set of criteria with which to evaluate their own governments.

Road Map of the Hypotheses and Following Chapters

In this chapter, I have introduced in detail the primary avenues through which the Internet influences political evaluations and satisfaction, its mirror-holding and window-opening functions. Chapter 3 explores potential limitations and criticisms of mirror-holding and window-opening.

Chapters 4 through 7 test the Internet's effect across a range of political evaluations. The primary hypothesis tested in this analysis considers the Internet's influence on individuals' satisfaction with the quality of democratic practices available in one's own nation. Although many of the countries included in this analysis are not full democracies, there are a number of reasons why this is an important test of the Internet's influence on meaningful political evaluations. First and foremost, recall that the vast majority of these countries do entertain some restricted number of democratic practices. For example, as discussed in chapter 1, each of the countries in this analysis holds some form of regular "elections" of government officials. Even though many external observers may take for granted that these elections are frequently shams, it is clear that citizens living in these countries often place value in them.

Moreover, as noted previously, even though the global community does not consider many of these countries to be democracies, their leaders nevertheless often glorify and propagandize their democratic virtues to their own populations. This is because many of these countries are, in fact, hybrid regimes (Levitsky & Way 2002), which pair authoritarian governance with some measure of democratic rules. Citizens living in these countries tend to value these limited democratic practices, and governance is simply easier when citizens can be coopted into the belief that their government is actually responsive to the needs and preferences of its citizenry.

It is the very disjuncture between how a government defines itself and how that same government's (un)democratic character is revealed online that is central to the Internet's effect on citizens' evaluations of their governments—the very evaluations that, in some instances, will encourage citizens to act and organize politically. Thus, democratic satisfaction is a meaningful component of citizens' evaluations of the degree to which they perceive their governments as effectively serving the interests and well-being of its population, shaping their satisfaction with that government accordingly.

Accordingly, I predict that individuals' satisfaction with democracy will hinge on the actual quality of democratic practices that are available in that nation. Whereas the Internet will increase satisfaction in advanced democracies, it will depress satisfaction in nations with weak democratic practices. This means that the Internet's influence on democratic satisfaction is primarily information-driven rather than some sort of affective or visceral response such as increased across-the board-satisfaction as a result of psychic gratification incurred from increased expressive capacity online.[5]

A conditional effect of Internet use on democratic satisfaction is supported by research conducted by Devra Moehler (2008), which found that offline participation in civic activity imparts information to individuals—the content of which then determines the direction of the resultant attitude change. In other words, she finds that participation can promote positive attitude change if the experience of participation provided individuals with information that reflected positively on their governments and civic realm. However, it can promote negative attitude change when that participation exposes citizens to negative information regarding their governments.

This has important parallels to the primary hypothesis tested in this book, which predicts that the Internet will have a contingent effect on satisfaction, conditioned by the actual quality of democratic practices available in that nation. However, the theoretical argument tested in this book diverges from Moehler's research in some notable directions, beginning with the independent variables tested in the analyses. Whereas Moehler's theory pertains specifically to information garnered from actual political participation offline, this book argues that the Internet imparts information that better reflects on the actual performance of that government, regardless of participation. Information can be derived from participation, but participation is not a necessary component of acquiring or distributing information online. This distinction is particularly relevant in nondemocratic countries, where opportunities to participate are severely limited.

An additional distinction between information gained from the Internet versus offline participation is that the Internet possesses a special capacity to serve as a platform to publicly document and aggregate instances of government malfeasance and failure at a national level. As discussed in chapter 1, past research demonstrates that individuals may be inclined to "morselize" private experiences. Thus, the information garnered from offline participation may not exist at a level of abstraction that is suitable to nationally oriented judgments of a government's performance. The ability to aggregate and document individual experiences (including those derived from participation) at a national level, therefore, is a particularly potent and unique component of Internet's mirror-holding effect on evaluations and, thus, on satisfaction.

However, the Internet's capacity to promote political participation both online and offline also means that Moehler's findings should take on increased significance in the Internet age. Mossberger, Tolbert, and McNeal found that "the Internet increases the likelihood of voting and civic engagement" (2008, 2). Additionally, Earl and Kimport detail the leveraged affordances provided by the Internet, which sharply reduce "costs for creating, organizing, and participating in protest" (2011, 10). Finally, a meta-analysis that reviewed thirty-eight Internet studies concluded that the Internet did have a positive, but small, effect on political engagement (Boulianne 2009). Therefore, not only does the Internet impart more information to individuals regardless of participation, but it may also make individuals more likely to participate as compared to a world without Internet, further amplifying the likelihood that individuals are exposed to information that causes them to update their evaluations of their government's performance.

Thus, in nations with weak democratic practices, individuals will become increasingly dissatisfied with those practices as a result of the Internet's providing more information about the shortcomings and failures of their government's practices and institutions as predicted by mirror-holding. Window-opening provides an additional channel through which Internet use will diminish satisfaction in these countries, thanks to its capacity to expose users to a more globally consistent metric with which to compare the quality of their own nations' democratic practices. This is significant since, as congruence theory posits, individuals' satisfaction with democracy is shaped by the terms through which they conceptualize democracy. And in the Internet age, national officials have relinquished some degree of control over defining the terms through which their populations conceptualize democracy.

At other end of the spectrum, in nations with strong democratic practices, I predict that Internet use will exert a positive effect on satisfaction that also can be attributed to both mirror-holding and window-opening. With regard to mirror-holding, recent research finds that using the Internet, and specifically visiting e-government sites—which 82 percent of American Internet users reported accessing in 2010 (Smith 2010)—increases individuals' trust in their government in advanced democracies as well as their perceptions of their government's responsiveness and effectiveness (Tolbert & Mossberger 2006; Welch et al. 2005; West 2004).

However, it is not simply accessing the e-government site itself that increased users' trust and perceptions of responsiveness. Rather, it is the capacity to communicate with elected representatives and increased access to information provided by e-government websites that drives this positive effect. Accordingly, Tolbert & Mossberger (2006) find that trust derived from e-government sites is *process-based,* which is "rooted in repeated exchanges or interactions with government. As a result of these interactions, individuals participate in instrumental exchanges and get what they need, but there are also symbolic exchanges . . . based on perceptions that government cares about citizens, their needs, and their expectations" (356).

Therefore, increased positive evaluations that derive from exposure to e-government sites in advanced democracies are a result of the positive information that citizens gain from these sites regarding how effectively their government functions. Simply putting up an e-government site in a country with weak democratic practices is unlikely to convey this positive experience and image of system responsiveness. Rather, if anything, it may reinforce citizens' awareness of the weaknesses of the democratic practices available in their countries by directly conveying information that highlights the absence of responsive institutions and transparency. Therefore, this positive effect of the Internet on evaluations of governments will be specific to advanced democracies.

Turning to window-opening, it is also likely that the comparative evaluations elicited by exposure to a more globally consistent metric of governance go both ways. Although it is certain that citizens living in advanced democracies harbor criticisms of their own governments as well as a sense of what could be improved or done better, exposure to more information about poorly performing governments in other nations nevertheless provides these individuals with a wider scope with which to evaluate their own government. The window provided by the Internet encourages users to consider their own government's performance relative to a fuller spectrum of the performance of other governments, thus increasing Internet users' satisfaction in nations ranked on the higher end of this spectrum.

Taken as a whole, these considerations lead to the primary hypothesis directing this research:

> **Hypothesis 1:** Internet use will increase satisfaction with democracy in nations boasting high-functioning democracies, but it will depress satisfaction in nations with poor democratic practices.

This hypothesis is tested in the chapters 4 through 6, which employ different methods and draw from different data sets at different levels of analysis. In chapter 4, I employ a random-effects regression analysis to test the effect of Internet penetration on satisfaction at the country level from 2004 to 2008. In chapter 5, I test this effect at the individual level by means of a multilevel analysis of cross-sectional survey data as well as an additional analysis employing a two-stage least-squares auxiliary variable.

Then, in chapter 6, I test this effect by means of a randomized field experiment in Bosnia, which provides a strong and direct test of the causal nature of this relationship. I also present additional findings from my field experiment in Bosnia, which explores the Internet's effect on a broader range of related evaluations. First, this includes whether the Internet causes individuals to reevaluate the quality of democratic practices available in their nation. This enables a test of whether Internet's effect on satisfaction is, in fact, information driven as opposed to being a more visceral effect or the result of across-the-board, indiscriminate cynicism and dissatisfaction prompted by Internet use. This leads to the following hypothesis:

> **Hypothesis 2:** Internet use encourages individuals to reevaluate the quality of democratic practices available in their country in the same direction as their change in satisfaction.

In chapter 6 I also test whether the Internet exposes individuals to a more globally consistent conception of what constitutes good democratic governance, one dominated by the norms commonly associated with advanced democracies. As predicted by window-opening, this is an important component of the Internet's capacity to influence democratic satisfaction because there are several different ways to conceptualize democracy (G. Almond & Verba 1963; Dalton et al. 2007). Moreover, congruence theory contends that satisfaction with democracy is contingent on individuals' beliefs about what actually constitutes democracy (Anderson & Guillory 1997; Kornberg & Clarke 1994; Miller et al. 1997). The capacity to define democracy is a crucial component in shaping support for democratic governments, particularly those in transition. Therefore, it is important to determine whether exposure to information about how democracy functions in the advanced democracies that dominate the Internet restricts a government's latitude in defining the terms through which its own citizens conceptualize and evaluate democratic practices in their own nations. Thus, I test the following hypothesis:

> **Hypothesis 3:** Internet users in a developing democracy will be more likely to conceptualize democracy in terms of the democratic rights and norms generally associated with advanced democracies.

Finally, in chapter 7, I report the findings of the field experiment conducted in Tanzania. Here, I test the Internet's influence on individuals' evaluations of a specific democratic process. Specifically, I test whether Internet use influenced their evaluation of the integrity of the 2010 presidential election and subsequent ballot recount in Tanzania. The history of protests, riots, and revolts precipitated by contested electoral results in democratizing nations renders this an important consideration of the Internet's capacity to alter the sort of evaluations that can prompt dissatisfaction and thereby potentially increase individuals' motivation to act and organize politically. To provide more insight into the full range of the Internet's effects in an electoral context, I also test a range of election-related evaluations and behaviors such as propensity to vote in the election and attend political meetings, as well as whether men and women were differently affected by Internet use.

Thus, the final hypothesis tested in this analysis:

> **Hypothesis 4:** Internet users will become more critical of specific government processes, such as elections, that do not meet democratic standards.

CHAPTER 3

Potential Limitations of Mirror-Holding and Window-Opening

THIS CHAPTER ADDRESSES prominent criticisms that potentially limit the influence of the Internet's mirror-holding and window-opening functions on the set of information and criteria that shape citizens' political evaluations and satisfaction. A primary potential limitation—government censorship—has already been effectively examined in chapter 2. However, five compelling potential limitations remain. These include: (1) to what degree governments can stifle critical content online through less overt cyber warfare; (2) to what degree state-sponsored propaganda or misinformation distorts the content individuals are exposed to online; (3) whether the digital divide severely circumscribes the Internet's influence; (4) whether mobile phones, as opposed to the Internet, really have the most meaningful impact in these countries; and (5) whether there is actually "too much choice" in content available online?

Cyber Warfare

While it is clear that critical information slips through the cracks of even the most sophisticated Internet regulatory systems, formalized censorship is not the only tool available to governments in their attempt to control or mitigate critical information available online. Another viable approach includes the government's deploying its own cyber army to identify, attack, and dismantle critical websites.

A prominent example of a government that has achieved relative success with this alternative approach is Russia, where there is no "official" Internet censorship system. Instead, as Morozov (2011a) reports, pro-Kremlin netizens actively monitor online content and attack websites and blogs that are deemed critical of the government. Another example comes from Venezuela, where prominent anti-Chavez activists regularly use Twitter to criticize the president. One such critic, soap opera writer Leonardo Padron, has built a following of roughly 250,000 Internet users. Recently, however, pro-Chavez cyber forces hijacked his Twitter account, turning the tables on Padron by tweeting disparaging messages about him through his own account. The group responsible for this cyber-attack, named N33, claims not to have any formal links to the Chavez government, but the veracity of this claim is unverifiable (Associated Press 2011). What is clear is that this less formal version of Internet control by vigilante types may be a potent alternative to formalized censorship.

In yet another example, hackers have been active on both sides of the Syrian uprising against President Assad. Anti-government activists have hacked into numerous government sites, posting interactive maps and accounts of government brutalities. However, pro-Assad forces have also used the Internet to further their cause. This group, calling themselves the Syrian Electronic Army, has used the Internet to attack the websites of perceived supporters of the rebellion, to post phone numbers and addresses of suspected opposition supporters, and to flood social websites with pro-Assad messages and post thinly veiled threats (Amos 2011; Karam 2011). Since 2011, the Syrian Electronic Army has also claimed responsibility for attacks on a multitude of news organization websites, including the *New York Times,* Al Jazeera, BBC, the *Guardian,* and the *Huffington Post.* Then, in September of 2013, visitors to the U.S. Marine Corps homepage were redirected to a page bearing a message from the Syrian Electronic Army that read, "Obama is a traitor who wants to put your lives in danger to rescue Al Qaeda insurgents. Marines, please take a look at what your comrades think about Obama's alliance with al-Qaeda against Syria" (Chalabi 2013).

So the question is: does this limit the Internet's mirror-holding function? Clearly, to some degree, it does. The government's use of the Internet to attack and intimidate critics likely discourages some number of present or would-be critics from posting their experiences and perspectives to the Internet. This limits the range and quantity of information available online compared to that which would be available if critics were not actively harassed and threatened. However, the abundant examples of the vibrant space that critical voices continue to occupy online in these same countries makes it clear that these intimidation tactics do not dissuade all critics. Moreover, the very extent to which governments have gone to fight these critics online and offline underscores the continued existence and potential impact of critical voices on the Internet. Thus, even if the situation is less than ideal, relative to a world without it, the Internet still provides a more nuanced mirror to citizens with which to reflect on the actual performance of their governments than do traditional media.

Finally, since these government-sponsored cyber-attacks—such as the arrest and imprisonment of prominent anti-government bloggers—are often visible to the public both online and offline, it is worthwhile to consider whether the attacks themselves provide Internet users with information regarding their government's treatment of its citizens. Basically, the very act of aggressively pursuing and attacking critical voices online contributes information about how the government treats its citizens and the extent of actual democratic practices available in that country. Thus, somewhat ironically, to some degree the attacks themselves counteract the government's goal of limiting the amount of information online that reflects poorly on the government's treatment of its citizens.

State-Sponsored Propaganda and Misinformation Online

Another viable alternative to more formalized censorship available to governments entails flooding the Internet with state-sponsored propaganda and misinformation in an attempt to drown out critical voices on the Internet. For example, much of Russia's primary Internet resources are owned by government-controlled or Kremlin-friendly companies and oligarchs. This facilitates the Kremlin's aggressive utilization of the Internet to "spread propaganda and bolster government popularity, sometimes with comical zeal" (Morozov 2011b).

Clearly, to some degree this does distort the content of the information that the Internet provides to individuals. However, while it may somewhat becloud the mirror and window provided by the Internet, it does not obscure either entirely for two important reasons. First, most of these governments pursued aggressive propaganda campaigns long before the Internet came along, so these populations have long been fed a steady diet of pro-government information. Therefore, the proper point of comparison is not the content of information online in a world where critics must compete with pro-government propaganda relative to some sort of ideal world of perfect information online that is completely free of distortion.[1] Rather, the meaningful comparison is the sort of information that the Internet, with all its shortcomings, provides to citizens relative to the sort of information that was available for public consumption before the Internet existed. Thus, considering the abundance of anecdotes documenting the continued presence of critical content online, the mirror and window provided by the Internet, although less than perfect and deliberately clouded at times by government propaganda, still provides a better reflection of how a government is actually performing than would be available in a world free of the Internet.

The second limitation of the capacity for state-sponsored propaganda and misinformation to completely obscure the mirror and window provided by the Internet is that in the long term it will simply become increasingly costly for states to sustain and prop up misinformation in the world of the Internet. Borrowing language from classic economic theories, as a result of the defining features of the Internet discussed previously, the Internet has so fundamentally changed the properties of information and its production that the production and dissemination of misinformation and propaganda based on falsehoods will be increasingly untenable for states over time. This is for two reasons: First, thanks to the Internet, it is now more efficient for individuals and entities outside of the government to produce and distribute information. This has to some degree privatized information production and dissemination, increasing the supply of information in countries where the means for public information production and dissemination were previously entirely or primarily under state control. Second, the efficiency with which information moves within and across borders has made information very fluid or, in economic terms, has increased the circulation of information flows within and across borders. This has contributed to the liberalization of information markets. Each of these changes has forced domestic state-run information markets, which were previously highly insulated, to open up to domestic and global competition in the production and dissemination of public information.

These changes have strong implications for the governments' ability to continue to shelter and prop up domestic state-run information markets because state-run markets, particularly those based on misinformation and propaganda, tend to be relatively inefficient. First, when states exclusively control the production and dissemination of information, this tends to result in a limited supply of information that generally cannot meet demand. Second, since some part of the information produced by these states is in the form of propaganda based on misinformation and falsehoods, the information supplied by state-run markets tends to be relatively costly to produce. This diverts state resources that could be spent elsewhere and exacerbates the productive inefficiency[2] of this market.

The reason that misinformation and propaganda are costly to produce is that they are not grounded on truth and thus cannot be verified objectively and empirically. Instead, the government must spend resources to create and then prop up mistruth by coopting or coercing individuals to corroborate misinformation and often even fabricate official "evidence" to support it. Moreover, states must often spend resources to suppress contradictory information based on actual events or truths, either through intimidation to ensure silence, through censorship, or through some sort of cover-up. This process of information production is costly in both time and resources. Thus, information supplied by state-run markets that is fabricated from misinformation and falsehoods tends to be characterized by productive inefficiency.

The cost of producing misinformation increases further when information becomes more fluid and the means for information production and dissemination becomes more privatized, since the state must now compete directly against non-state actors in the course of producing and distributing information. State-run information markets that supply misinformation are further disadvantaged when they have to compete against suppliers of veracious information because truth is simply more efficient to produce and distribute since it is verifiable. Not only is supporting evidence already available through actual observation and empirical confirmation, but it also does not require the coercion of individuals to corroborate it (or at least to suppress contradictory information) or the fabrication of supporting evidence.

Thus, government misinformation and propaganda, which has always existed and now also exists online, simply constitutes a less efficient information market than information markets consisting of veracious information. As the number of producers and suppliers of information increases, thanks to the Internet, information becomes further privatized, and markets further liberalize due to more fluid information flows. As a result, domestic state-run information markets become less sheltered from competition, both domestic and global. In such a world, it will be increasingly difficult for state-run information markets, which are generally unable to satisfy existing demand and are characterized by productive inefficiency, to remain competitive. Thus, just as capital flows in to correct financial market inefficiencies, veracious information flows in to correct inefficient state-run information markets that fabricate information from falsehoods. Over time, this will further limit the degree to which state propaganda and misinformation online will becloud the mirror and window provided by the Internet.

The Digital Divide

The term *digital divide* originated in the mid-1990s to refer to the divide separating those with and without computer access. The term then evolved with technology in order to incorporate access to the Internet and, more recently, to broadband technology. While the actual technologies straddling the divide have shifted over the past decades, the essential meaning and significance of the term remains unchanged. It represents the stark difference in access to information, education and employment opportunities, and tools of political participation that differentiate those with from those without access to digital technology.

A seminal work about the Internet's digital divide is Pippa Norris's *Digital Divide: Civic Engagement, Information Poverty, and the Internet Worldwide* (2001). Norris delineates and expands on three types of meaningful divides: (1) the social divide within countries between those with and without access, (2) the global divide between countries with more and less access, and (3) the political divide between those who use the Internet toward political ends and those who do not.

As of 2013, a large global divide still exists. Although Internet penetration reached 75 percent in Europe, 61 percent in the Americas, 38 percent in Arab States, and 32 percent in Asia and the Pacific, Africa continued to lag far behind at 16 percent (ITU 2013). Furthermore, a significant social divide still persists, particularly within countries with lower Internet penetration rates. In these countries, men with more education and from higher socioeconomic backgrounds tend to be the most likely to be online (Christensen & Levinson 2003; ITU 2013). In addition to the monetary costs associated with using the Internet, this persistent digital divide within nations can be further explained by differences in education, literacy, and technical skills (Mossberger, Kaplan, & Gilbert 2008).

To some degree, these divides do limit the effects of mirror-holding and window-opening on political evaluations, as a result of constraining the number of individuals exposed to information online. However, once again, the proper point of comparison is between a world without the Internet and the world with the Internet as it exists—divides and all—as opposed to some sort of ideal world of universal Internet access. Even if only 16 percent of the African population is exposed to the more robust and diverse set of information provided by the Internet, this is still a meaningful increase in the number of individuals exposed to such information. Therefore, although the effects of mirror-holding and window-opening may be somewhat diminished by these divides, they are not entirely obscured.

There are also the positive externalities that Internet use bestows upon societies, described by Mossberger, Tolbert, and McNeal as the "social benefits beyond those reaped by the individuals who use the technology" (2008, 3). This means that the availability of a greater volume of more diverse information online benefits more citizens than those who physically access that information. To illustrate the positive externalities of the Internet for political participation, Mossberger, Tolbert, and McNeal explain that "information available online helps citizens to be more informed about politics and more inclined to participate, then society as a whole profits from broader and possibly more deliberative participation in democratic processes" (2008, 3).

It is also evident that information acquired online does not exist only online. That is, information acquired online is easily and often communicated to a broader audience through offline channels, thus updating the classic theory of the two-step flow of information. While recent research suggests that the two-step flow may no longer be widely applicable in information-rich societies (W. L. Bennett & Manheim 2006), it remains relevant in more information-scarce countries.

First articulated by Katz and Lazarsfeld in 1955 in reference to traditional media, the two-step flow theory of information posits that information attained from the mass media tends to move in two stages. In the first stage, opinion leaders are exposed to political information directly from the mass media. In the second stage, these opinion leaders pass this information on, often accompanied by their own interpretation, to those they interact with directly in their various social networks. Thus, even in countries with limited Internet exposure, it is likely that some degree of the information attained online is diffused by Internet users to nonusers in their social networks. This also means that individuals who either cannot afford or do not have the literacy or technical skills to use the Internet are still exposed to some portion of the greater volume of information that the Internet provides.

Additionally, a study by Mossberger, Kaplan, and Gilbert (2008) demonstrates that individuals living in areas of concentrated poverty are motivated to seek out Internet access despite lacking access at home or work: "Some good news for closing technology gaps is clearly evident. . . . as some of those who lack regular access are still willing and able to go online at times" (485). While these researchers issue the caveat that motivation to find alternative access to the Internet in communities of concentrated poverty is moderated by education levels and supportive social networks, these findings nevertheless somewhat allay concerns about digital divide in communities where individuals largely lack Internet access at home or work.

Finally, mobile phones will increasingly further help to bridge the divide between those with computer-based Internet access and those without. First and foremost, mobile phones make it more efficient for opinion leaders to disseminate the information they receive online to their own social networks. Additionally, several Internet websites and applications are available through mobile phones. Not only does this grant access to specific Internet-based content to individuals without actual computer access, but VoIP (Voice over Internet Protocol) further enables individuals who would have otherwise been excluded due to illiteracy to access some degree of Internet-based content. According to Essounggou (2010), "Africans are coupling their already extensive use of cell phones with a more recent and massive interest in social media—Internet-based tools and platforms that allow people to interact with each other much more than in the past. In the process, Africans are leading what may be the next global trend: a major shift to mobile Internet use, with social media as its main drivers."

Mobile Phones versus Computers

Taking into consideration the previous discussion, one may wonder whether it might actually be mobile phones that are having a more meaningful impact in many of these countries. To be sure, mobile phones are substantially more ubiquitous than computers—in Africa, mobile phone subscription penetration has reached 63 percent as of 2013 (ITU 2013). A number of recent studies substantiate the myriad ways that mobile phones have streamlined and facilitated day-to-day life on the continent. For example, mobile phones have contributed to reduced price discrepancies (Aker 2008), increased consumer and producer welfare (Abraham 2007; Jensen 2007), improved productivity (Donner 2006; Lane et al. 2006; Moloney 2005) and assistance in finding employment (Frost & Sullivan 2006; Samuel et al. 2005), as well as positively affected election monitoring and the efficient provision of health care resources (Livingston 2011) and reduced levels of perceived corruption (Bailard 2009).

So, is it really mobile phones that are having the more meaningful impact in these countries? I argue that in the world of increased convergence (in which previously distinct media industries increasingly share content, functions, audiences, platforms, etc.) such a determination need not exist. In a world where individuals are increasingly using mobile phones to access and contribute to Internet content, how should the credit for this be divided between computers and mobile phones?

While the Internet may have originated as a network that connected computers and may still be primarily accessed through computers in developed countries, the Internet and its capacity to reshape contemporary information landscapes is not confined only to computers. As technologies continue to converge, and more technologies emerge that enable Internet

access (such as tablets and iPads), the Internet as a network of information and communication will be less confined to and defined by computer
use: "The set of technologies known throughout most of the 1990s as 'the
Internet' is steadily merging with other technologies. . . . As these technologies continue to evolve, what is actually 'the Internet' will become less clear
and less important. The fundamental modes of communication that various
technologies enable will become more crucial than the machinery involved"
(Bimber 2003, 8).

Thus, for present purposes it is less important which technology individuals are physically using to access Internet-based content. What matters
more is that they can use *any* technology to access and contribute to the
changing information landscapes that characterize the current information
revolution in which the Internet plays a foundational role. Mobile phones
certainly have their own place in this landscape, and to some degree their
own unique uses and contributions to online information, but it is simply
too difficult to separate the effects of computer-based Internet use from that
of mobile phone–based Internet use. For example, how do you differentiate
information attained online by opinion leaders, which is then communicated by those opinion leaders via mobile phones to their social networks?
Or what if an individual takes a picture with his mobile phone, later posts it
to the Internet, and then communicates about that picture through Twitter
and Facebook?

Fortunately, there is no need to differentiate. Mobile phones and computer-
based Internet use are not mutually exclusive components of the revolution
currently reshaping the information landscapes within and across countries.
As Manuel Castells explains, information and communication technologies
do not exist or operate in isolation from one another: "Each leap and bound
in a specific technological field amplifies the effects of related information
technologies. Thus, mobile telephony, relying on computing power to route
the messages, provides at the same time the basis for ubiquitous computing and for real-time, untethered, interactive electronic communication"
(1996, 46).

Any attempt to discuss or study the effects of Internet access through mobile phones as opposed to computer-based Internet use would be a frustrat-
ing and ultimately futile endeavor, since "trends point to a future in which
more and more aspects of communication become dependent upon the Internet" (Chadwick 2006, 8). Accordingly, my focus on the Internet does
not imply any preference for or separation between computer-based and
mobile phone–based Internet access. Instead, I subscribe to the definition of
the Internet provided by Andrew Chadwick in *Internet Politics:* "a network

of networks of one-to-one, one-to-many, many-to-many, and many-to-one local, national, and global information and communication technologies with relatively open standards and protocols and comparatively low barriers to entry" (2006, 7).

Too Much Choice Online?

The proliferation of media outlets has sparked concern about the potentially deleterious consequences of "too much choice" among media content for audiences. Specifically, motivated by the theory of selective exposure (Zillman & Bryant 1985), which contends that individuals prefer to expose themselves to information that reinforces rather than challenges their pre-existing attitudes and opinions, some scholars argue that the proliferation in media options (particularly that of cable television and the Internet) may be further polarizing the American population (Sunstein 2001; Stroud 2008). Others argue that this multiplication of media choices is increasingly leading to the fragmentation of audiences, such that it will be difficult to focus and sustain public attention around a specific set of issues (Tewksbury 2005; Tewksbury & Rittenberg 2009)—a particular problem for representative democracies, where elected leaders are expected to be responsive to the public's preferences and agenda.[3]

Although these are legitimate concerns, they have received mixed empirical support, with some studies showing marginal or nonexistent fragmentation and polarization resulting from online news consumption (Coleman & McCombs 2007; Webster & Ksiazek 2012). For example, Gentzkow and Shapiro (2011) compare face-to-face interactions, traditional media consumption, and Internet use and find no support for the argument that Internet users are highly ideologically polarized and segregated in the websites they visit. They attribute this to their finding that the majority of Internet users tend to visit more centrist and moderate websites and also tend to visit multiple websites when gathering news. Moreover, they found that exposure to content online was markedly less ideologically segregated than the respondents' face-to-face interactions—in other words, getting online exposed individuals to a more diverse set of information than they tend to encounter in day-to-day interactions offline.

However, there is one remaining concern regarding the deleterious effects of "too much choice" that could prove problematic for the theoretical framework guiding this analysis: the degree to which the proliferation in media choice enables entertainment-seeking audiences to avoid news and political information altogether. Markus Prior, the most prominent scholar working within this line of inquiry, argues that "greater choice allows politically interested people to access more information and increase their political knowledge. Yet those who prefer nonpolitical content can more easily escape the news and therefore pick up less political information than they used to" (2005, 577). Employing panel survey data of respondents living in the United States, Prior finds that among individuals who express an interest in news, cable television and Internet use increase political knowledge; however, among those who report a strong preference for entertainment content, these media decrease their political knowledge over time.

Clearly, if some individuals are using the Internet to effectively avoid political information and news content, this could circumscribe the effects of mirror-holding and window-opening on the information and expectations that individuals employ to evaluate their government. However, there are two aspects of this line of inquiry that limit its relevance to mirror-holding and window-opening and thus limit the degree to which Prior's findings apply to the present analysis. Specifically, these include when and where this research was conducted.

First, Prior's analysis employs data that was collected between 2000 and 2003, before the advent of social media such as Facebook and Twitter, which have become staples of present-day Internet use across the globe. As of 2013, there were more than one billion active Facebook users from well over two hundred countries (Internet World Stats 2012; Tam 2013). Moreover, as discussed in chapter 2, there is compelling evidence substantiating some degree of incidental exposure to news content on social media websites, which are often frequented by entertainment-seeking Internet users. More generally, the shape and content of the Internet has changed considerably in the past several years, and as a result, analyses of data from the turn of the century do not systematically test the likelihood of incidental news exposure during entertainment-seeking online in a context that is representative of today's online environment. Moreover, more recent research confirms incidental exposure to news content during the course of Internet use, particularly in the course of entertainment and sports news seeking (Lee 2009).

Second, Prior's study was conducted in a developed country that was already relatively information-abundant compared to information availability in developing nations. Thus, making generalizations across these very different information environments would be problematic. However, for the sake of argument, even if these results were generalizable across very different milieus, Prior's finding that news-oriented audiences increase their political knowledge as a result of Internet use actually becomes a particularly persuasive piece of evidence in support of mirror-holding and window-opening.

If one assumes that a certain portion of citizens in these countries are interested in accessing news content[4] and that previous to the Internet, the amount and range of information available was highly limited and controlled by the state, then access to the more abundant and varied content online has particularly large consequences for the news-seeking individuals living in these countries. But, what about the entertainment-seekers in these countries? Even putting aside incidental exposure to political information on social media and more general Internet use, quite simply it may not be necessary to establish that all citizens online intentionally consume news in order to observe a measurable effect of political information acquired online on aggregate public opinion. If, for instance, one-third of a country's population is online (approximately the percentage of individuals in developing countries that were online as of 2013 according to the International Telecommunications Union) and only one-third of those are inclined to seek political information online, any resultant change in the evaluations and satisfaction of this segment of a nation's citizenry would still have real and measurable ramifications. Moreover, thanks to the two-step flow of information (Katz & Lazarsfeld 1955), which remains relevant in developing countries (particularly those where illiteracy is still an issue, as discussed in chapter 2), it is likely that some portion of the information acquired online by a minority of news-seekers diffuses to a larger network of peers—including entertainment-seekers—thus, shifting evaluations and satisfaction accordingly.

In summary, "too much choice" among online content falls short of posing a formidable challenge to mirror-holding and window-opening. First, there is mounting evidence that even entertainment-seekers are incidentally exposed to political information online to some degree, particularly through the ubiquitous use of social media across the globe. Second, it is clear that there are a number of users who do turn to the Internet specifically to search out political information. This should not be surprising, particularly in countries where traditional media strictly circumscribed the amount and type of information available for public consumption. Where there is limited protection of political rights, where the rule of law is tenuous, and where one's life can be affected quite suddenly and profoundly by the decisions of those in power, political information takes on added significance. Thus, when consequences can be great and information is limited, the value of even a marginal increase in political information may be enough to motivate news-seeking behavior online. In this context, too much choice online may actually enhance the capacity for mirror-holding and window-opening to expose a meaningful segment of Internet users to a more diverse set of information, thus shaping their evaluations and satisfaction accordingly.

Summary and Conclusion

This chapter discussed five potential limitations to the capacity for mirror-holding and window-opening to expose individuals to information that influence their evaluations of their governments. These limitations include concerns regarding whether governments can employ cyber warfare to effectively squash critical content online, whether state-sponsored propaganda and misinformation distort the information individuals are exposed to online, whether the digital divide severely limits the Internet's influence, whether mobile phones are actually the technology that is having the most meaningful impact in these countries, and whether there is actually too much choice between content online.

Although it is clear that each of these concerns does somewhat limit mirror-holding and window-opening to varying degrees across different countries, it is also clear that their capacity to obscure or becloud the mirror and window provided by the Internet is conscribed. Thus, even in countries with governments pursuing active cyber warfare or propaganda online, or in countries with stark digital divides, or in countries with vastly more mobile phones than computers, it remains the case that markedly more information is available to these citizens than would be available in a world without the Internet.

This, after all, is the proper point of comparison: it is not the Internet as it currently exists compared to a world of perfect and complete information online. Rather, it is the Internet as it exists, limitations and all, compared to the information landscapes that existed before the Internet. For this reason, in spite of these limitations, the Internet still provides individuals with more information about their own governments as well as about governments across the globe than was previously available. And it is this information that influences citizens' evaluations of and satisfaction with their own governments.

CHAPTER 4

Determining the Effect of Internet Use on Democratic (Dis)Satisfaction

The Country Level

THIS CHAPTER tests the Internet's effect on democratic satisfaction at the country level in seventy-three nations spanning five continents. In this analysis, I employ a random effects regression to test the effect of Internet penetration on the percentage of citizens satisfied with how democracy functions in their own nation over a five-year period from 2004 through 2008. This approach provides a more rigorous test of this relationship than analyses of data from a single slice in time because it enables the analysis to determine whether changes in a nation's level of Internet penetration predicts changes in the level of democratic satisfaction over the same period of time.

In building this model, logic dictates that a range of factors influence both a nation's access to the Internet and its citizens' evaluations of their government's democratic performance. Accordingly, this analysis controls for the most prominent factors correlated with both Internet penetration and democratic satisfaction, including education, economic and living standards, press freedom, governmental effectiveness, and the actual quality of democratic practices available in that nation.

In the following sections, I describe the variables used in this analysis, discuss the advantages and appropriateness of a random effects model for testing this relationship, and report the results of the primary regression. I conclude with an additional regression to test the robustness of my results, in which I substitute the original variable measuring strength of democracy provided by the World Bank with alternative measures of strength of democracy provided by Freedom House.

The advantages of these additional tests are twofold. First, if the same relationship holds with distinct measures of democracy, this strengthens the empirical foundation for the relationship shared by Internet use and (dis)satisfaction. Second, since Freedom House provides two measures of two distinct types of democratic practices—political rights and civil liberties—it is possible to test whether either of these specific subsets of democratic features more strongly conditions the effect of Internet use on (dis)satisfaction. In other words, to what degree does the protection of civil liberties drive the effect of Internet use on satisfaction relative to the presence of durable democratic institutions? Answering this question will provide additional insight into the effect of mirror-holding and window-opening on political evaluations.

The Variables

This analysis controls for several factors that are correlated with both the level of Internet penetration in a nation and how (dis)satisfied citizens in those countries are with their governments. The first variable, education, better prepares citizens to operate technology (Horrigan 2006), suggesting that better education systems are correlated with expanded Internet penetration. It is also likely that a better education system influences citizens' opinions about their democracy, since education shapes individuals' understanding of and capacity to evaluate democracy. Baviskar and Malone (2004) find that education, and to a lesser degree income, shape individuals' conceptions of democracy, so that they are more likely to understand democracy in terms of means rather than ends. These different conceptions, they contend, encourage different evaluations of the development of a nation's democracy. Improved economic conditions also imply that citizens enjoy a higher level of material and financial comfort, which influence both attitudes toward democracy (Bratton & Mattes 2001) and affordability of Internet access via personal devices (e.g., computers, mobile phones, tablets) or Internet cafes. To control for the potentially confounding influences of education and economic standards, then, the model includes a variable measuring each nation's Human Development Index (HDI).[1] HDI is a composite index constructed by the United Nations Human Development Programme, which takes into account a nation's literacy rate, school enrollment, life expectancy, and GDP per capita.[2]

A free press is logically associated with a government's tolerance for the collection and dissemination of information for public consumption. This implies that the governments in nations with freer presses would also be less likely to actively stifle citizens' access to the Internet. Additionally, a free press is likely to provide a distinct set of information to citizens—relative to countries with censored press—which likely influences how citizens evaluate their governments. To control for the correlates of press freedom, therefore, the analysis also includes the Press Freedom Index (PFI) compiled by Freedom House,[3] thereby helping to separate the traditional press's effect from the independent effect of the Internet. The Press Freedom Index is derived from forty-three criteria that measure instances of press freedom violations toward individual journalists (e.g., murders, imprisonment, harassment) as well as at the institutional level (e.g., censorship, confiscation). These criteria also measure the impunity enjoyed by those that commit such violations as well as the degree of self-censorship by members of the news media.

The model also employs two governance indicators in order to gauge actual government performance in domains that likely contribute to both citizens' satisfaction with democracy and Internet penetration rates. First, in order to get an accurate picture of whether citizens' attitudes are enhanced or diminished by the Internet beyond the actual democratic functioning of the government itself, it is necessary to account for the strong correlation shared by Internet diffusion and democracy (Kedzie 1997; Milner 2006). I thus include the Voice and Accountability (VA) variable, which is the World Bank's index of a nation's quality of democracy. The World Bank (2011) describes its VA indicator as including "a number of indicators measuring various aspects of the political process, civil liberties, political and human rights, measuring the extent to which citizens of a country are able to participate in the selection of governments."

The second World Bank governance indicator is Governmental Effectiveness (GE), which gauges how well the government carries out the various tasks of governance, including the efficiency of government bureaucracies, the provision of public goods, and the successful implementation of policies. This variable accounts for the possibility that a government that is better able to carry out the task of governance is also more likely to successfully develop and provide Internet technology to its citizens as well as more likely to elicit positive evaluations from its citizenry in general.[4]

The independent variable of interest, Internet Penetration Rates, is built from data provided by the International Telecommunications Union (ITU). Based on country surveys and estimates derived from the number of Internet subscribers, this variable represents the estimated percentage of a nation's population between the ages of 15 and 74 that use the Internet in a given year. In 2004, across the countries in this analysis, Internet penetration ranged from a low of 2 percent in Nicaragua to a high of 82 percent in Sweden. The mean level of Internet penetration during 2004 was 30 percent, with a median of 25 percent Internet penetration and a standard deviation of 22 percent. By 2008, the mean level of Internet penetration of the countries included in this analysis increased to 34 percent, with a median of 31 percent and a standard deviation of 27 percent.[5]

In addition, since it is necessary to determine whether the Internet's influence on democratic satisfaction is contingent on the actual quality of democracy that a citizen enjoys, as Hypothesis 1 predicts, I also include an interaction term of Internet penetration and the World Bank's quality of democracy indicator (Internet Penetration Rate × Voice and Accountability). This enables the direction of the Internet's effect to vary according to the actual strength of democracy in that nation, as the theory guiding this analysis requires.

The dependent variable—Satisfaction with Democracy—is drawn from the four cross-sectional international survey organizations constituting the Globalbarometer series, which encompass the responses of individuals living in seventy-three countries spanning five different continents. Specifically, these surveys include the Latinobarometer, the Afrobaromter, the Eurobarometer, and the East-Asian Barometer. (See appendix 4.2 for the list of countries included.) In each of these surveys, respondents are asked their degree of satisfaction with the way that democracy functions in their country. To answer, they can choose from the following response options: Very satisfied, Fairly satisfied, Not very satisfied, or Not at all satisfied. The variable is calculated as the percentage of respondents in each country that answered that they were either fairly or very satisfied.

It is worthwhile to note that, since these surveys were implemented by four different organizations, each polling respondents in multiple different countries, there are slight differences in the wording employed in each analysis. However, a comparison of the questions reveals that these differences in wording are rather superficial. More importantly, since this analysis employs time-series cross-sectional data, the negligible differences across these surveys are offset by the ability to test this relationship over time within these countries. Thus, the consistency of the wording in each of the surveys used in each of the countries during the five years included in this analysis further allays any internal validity concerns that may derive from utilizing data collected by multiple survey organizations.

The Model

Since the mid-1980s, social scientists (particularly those in political science and microeconomics) have increasingly embraced regression models that permit the analysis of relationships simultaneously across units and over time. In other words, rather than study a single case over time (i.e., time-series) or a set of cases at one slice in time (i.e., cross-sectional), there has been a move toward models that enable researchers to analyze a set of cases over a period of time. Not only is this often theoretically more appropriate to the sort of questions we would like to answer, but such an approach is also considered more robust than analyses that only test a relationship in a static, single point in time.

In the words of James A. Stimson, an early pioneer of such models, this can be an "extraordinarily robust research design, allowing the study of causal dynamics across multiple cases. . . . Many of the threats to valid inference are specific to either cross-section or time-serial design, and many of them can be jointly controlled by incorporating both space and time in the analysis" (1985, 916). Accordingly, this chapter employs a time-series cross-sectional approach by means of a random effects model, in which I test the relationship shared by Internet penetration and (dis)satisfaction across seventy-three countries over a five-year period, from 2004 through 2008.

There is some question as to whether random effects models or fixed effects models are preferable for the analysis of time-series cross-sectional data. However, the theoretical framework guiding this analysis renders a random effects model as the more appropriate test for this specific analysis in substantive terms. Moreover, the results of a Hausman Test comparing these two models (the generally accepted means to determine whether a random effects or fixed effects model is more appropriate) substantiates the random effects model as the statistically preferable approach.

In more detail, whereas random effects models employ an estimator derived from a weighted average of fixed and between effects, the fixed effects estimator employs only the weighted average of the fixed effects. This means that, while fixed effects considers only within-country variation, random effects takes into account both within-country variation and between-country variation. Due to the window-opening function of the Internet—which I argue induces comparative evaluations of democratic performance by exposing individuals to information about how democracy functions in other nations—between-country variation is an integral component of the theory driving this analysis, which only a random effects model enables.

In addition, random effects are appropriate when the observations included in the analysis are considered a sample of a larger population, while fixed effects treat the observations as an exhaustive list of the population itself. Since my analysis incorporates a sample of seventy-three countries out of the entire population of nearly two hundred countries across this globe, the former assumption is clearly more appropriate for the present analysis. Additionally, random effects models are considered more efficient than fixed effects models, which provide very little efficiency in variables that vary only marginally within each group (as is the case for many of the variables in this analysis). Random effects models are also more efficient because they provide greater degrees of freedom (Baltagi 2008).

On the other hand, random effects models are problematic when the explanatory variables are correlated with the model's error term (i.e., residuals), which is often the case in social science research and which produces biased estimators. In addition, unlike random effects models, fixed effects models control for unobservable or immeasurable country-level factors that do not vary over time, minimizing the threat of omitted variable bias. On the other hand, fixed effects models do not allow for tests of time-invariant characteristics, such as factors that derive from regional membership.

Taken as a whole, although each specification has its own set of disadvantages, both theoretical and methodological specifications of this analysis render random effects as the more appropriate model. Additionally, the Hausman test, which tests whether a more efficient model (i.e., random effects) will still give consistent results when compared to a less efficient but consistent specification (i.e., fixed effects), is the generally accepted means to determine whether a random effects or fixed effects model is more appropriate (Hausman 1978). If the null hypothesis (i.e., the differences between the coefficients generated by each of these models are not systematic) cannot be rejected, then a random effects model is preferable since, in addition to being more efficient, this specification does not lose the information derived from between-country variation that is central to the theory driving this analysis. Running the Hausman test on my mode, the null hypothesis cannot be rejected at the 95 percent confident level (p-value = .26). Thus, a random effects model is the preferable model for this analysis.

The Results

For citizens living in nations with democratic practices ranked in approximately the top quartile over this five-year period, increased Internet penetration positively influences the percentage of citizens who are satisfied with their nation's democracy. However, Internet penetration wields the opposite influence on democratic satisfaction in nations ranked in the bottom three quartiles. In substantive terms, holding the other variables at their means, the marginal effects of increasing Internet penetration by a total of 25 percentage points over this five-year period predicts a 6 percentage

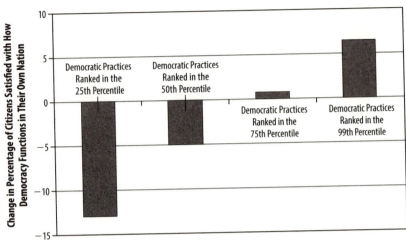

FIGURE 4.1 Average Marginal Effect of 25-percentage-point Increase in Internet Penetration on Democratic Satisfaction

point increase in the number of satisfied citizens living in a nation ranked in the 99th percentile (in terms of strength of democratic practices). Conversely, satisfaction rates declined by nearly 13 percentage points in nations ranked in the 25th percentile when Internet penetration increased by the same amount (see figure 4.1). Moreover, plotting the 95 percent confidence intervals of the average marginal effects of the interaction terms indicates significant and clear differential effects of Internet penetration on satisfaction in countries with democratic practices ranked below the 60th percentile and above the 90th percentile. Statistics from the International Telecommunications Union (ITU 2013) underscore the tangible consequences of the size of these effects: whereas 77 percent of individuals in the developed world used the Internet in 2013, in developing countries nearly 1 in 3 individuals were online as of this same year. This means that Internet penetration rates across the globe have already reached levels where we will see meaningful and tangible effects of Internet use on democratic satisfaction.

These findings support the interactive effect of the Internet predicted by the mirror-holding and window-opening functions, confirming Hypothesis 1 at the .01 significance level. While the growth in Internet access from 2004 to 2008 increased the percentage of citizens that were satisfied with their democracy in nations boasting top-ranked democracies, it depressed democratic satisfaction among citizens living in nations with weaker democratic practices.[6] (See table A4.1 for the results of this regression. Note that all regression tables for this chapter are included in appendix 4.1.) Additionally, in order to test the robustness of these results, I ran a number of additional regressions with various combinations of the control variables omitted, and the results remain largely commensurate (see table A4.2).

Alternative Democracy Variable

To further test the robustness of the primary regression results, I employ Freedom House's democracy measures in place of the democracy measure provided by the World Bank (VA) that was included in the primary regression. Freedom House's democracy measures consist of two distinct democratic categories: political rights (FHPR) and civil liberties (FHCL). Whereas the political rights index takes into account institutions and rights that enable citizens to participate freely in the political process—such as the right to vote, the accountability of elected officials, the right to form political parties, and the ability to impact policy—the civil liberties index focuses on the strength and protection of individual's rights, such as freedom of expression and belief, personal autonomy, and the right to organize. These indexes are coded on a 1 to 7 scale, with 1 being the highest score a nation's democracy can be awarded and 7 being the lowest. Dozens of analysts and advisors contribute to the construction of these scores, taking into account "a broad range of sources of information—including foreign and domestic news reports, academic analyses, nongovernmental organizations, think tanks, individual professional contacts, and visits to the region" (Freedom House 2012).

In the first regression, I replace the World Bank's democracy measure (VA) with Freedom House's measure of civil liberties (FHCL), yielding a remarkably similar relationship between Internet penetration and democratic satisfaction (see table A4.3). While expanded Internet penetration correlates with enhanced democratic satisfaction in nations ranked in the Freedom House's highest category of democratic performance (1), the relationship is nearly flat for countries ranked in second highest category (2), and Internet penetration depresses satisfaction in nations with democracies ranked below this threshold (3 to 7).

Admittedly, the relationship drops in significance to the .1 level. But this is to be expected, considering the substantial loss of information that accompanies replacing the World Bank's measure with the Freedom House measure. Whereas World Bank's indicator ranks countries between 1 and 100 (to the tenth unit), the Freedom House measure compresses all countries into a 7-category scale, severely restricting the nuance and specificity of this measure. Therefore, the finding that the relationship between

Internet penetration and democratic satisfaction so closely mirrors that in the original analysis in substantive terms—as well as maintaining statistical significance despite this substantial loss of information—further validates the Internet's contingent effect on democratic satisfaction.

However, whereas the Internet's contingent effect on democratic satisfaction is largely commensurate with the primary regression when Freedom House's civil liberties index is incorporated into the model, the strength of these correlations shrinks somewhat in both substantive and statistical significance when the political rights variable is substituted into the model instead (see table A4.4). In consideration of these results, it appears that the Internet's capacity to influence citizens' satisfaction with how democracy functions in their country may hinge more on the presence and protection of civil liberties in that country than on the existence of more institutional and procedurally oriented components of democracy. This is compatible with the theory of the Internet's mirror-holding and window-opening functions, since information about a government's protection of (or failure to protect) civil liberties is likely much more straightforward and tangible—and therefore more transmissible via the Internet—than the somewhat more arcane and esoteric aspects of its political institutions and procedures.

Conclusion

The primary hypothesis driving this analysis—that the Internet exerts an interactive influence on democratic satisfaction, conditioned by the actual quality of democratic practices available in a nation—garnered considerable support from the country-level analyses in this chapter. The primary regression, which incorporates time-series cross-sectional data from seventy-three countries during a five-year period, reveals that the Internet has a significant and substantively meaningful effect on democratic satisfaction, reaching the .01 significance level. Whereas increased Internet penetration increased satisfaction in nations with robust democratic practices, it depressed satisfaction in nations with weaker democratic practices.

In addition to several tests of robustness, I ran additional regressions with two alternate measures of strength of democracy provided by Freedom House. Besides supporting the findings produced by the primary model, these additional tests suggest that the Internet's effect may be more dependent on the quality of civil rights protection available in a country than on the strength of more structural and institutional democratic features. This is an important and not counterintuitive finding—after all, information about specific civil rights abuses can be conveyed much more succinctly and vividly in an online forum than information highlighting more diffuse and systemic procedural and bureaucratic inadequacies of various government institutions. Future research should seek to flesh out the relative influence of these two types of democratic features more thoroughly.

In conclusion, an important implication of the interactive effect of the Internet on satisfaction is that the Internet is unlikely to produce uniform effects on political attitudes across different countries. This has relevance for the determinist versus social constructionist debate regarding technology's impact. While technological determinists contend that the social uses and effects of a technology are determined by the structure of the technology itself, constructionists maintain that the use and effects of technology are rooted in and driven by its social context. By substantiating the Internet's strong interactive relationship with democratic satisfaction, the findings of this analysis clearly lend weight to the constructionist view. Therefore, it is likely that only testing for uniform effects across countries will lead researchers to overlook or fail to detect important components of the Internet's influence.

Finally, what do these findings imply about the Internet's influence on the process of democratization in general? The finding that Internet exposure makes individuals less satisfied with sub-par democratic practices seems to bode well for democratization. However, more critical evaluations do not necessarily or automatically translate into across-the-board gains in democratic attitudes and behavior. Thus, as shown by findings reported in the following chapters, it may be prudent for Internet enthusiasts to temper their zeal until future analyses further reveal and explore the political, social, historical, and economic contexts that likely condition the Internet's effect across borders.

Appendix 4.1. Regression Results

TABLE A 4.1. Country-level regression of percentage of citizens satisfied with how democracy functions in their own nation, 2004 through 2008

	Slope	Standard Error	95% CI	p-value
Internet Penetration Rate (0–1 range, mean = 0.33, sd = 0.19)	−0.69	0.26	[−1.19, −0.09]	≤0.008***
Voice and Accountability (0–1 range, mean = 0.67, sd = 0.22)	0.08	0.17	[−0.25, 0.4]	≤0.64
Interaction of Internet Penetration Rate and Voice and Accountability (0–1 range, mean = 0.26, sd = 0.25)	0.95	0.3	[0.36, 1.5]	≤0.002***
Human Development Index (0–1 range, mean = 0.8,1 sd = 0.14)	0.51	0.23	[0.06, 0.95]	≤0.03**
Press Freedom Index (0–1 range, mean = 0.67, sd = 0.18)	−0.05	0.08	[−0.22, 0.11]	≤0.53
Governmental Effectiveness (0–1 range, mean = 0.63, sd = 0.23)	0.23	0.13	[−0.02, 0.49]	≤0.07*
Intercept	0.002	0.2		
Number of observations: 246 Number of countries: 73 Average number of observations per country: 3.4 Adjusted r-squared overall: 57%				

Note. CI = confidence interval. Dependent variable is the percentage of citizens that are fairly or highly satisfied with their nation's quality of democracy, scored to a continuous 0–1 range. It has a mean of 0.49 and a standard deviation (sd) of 0.19. For brevity's sake, the region-dummy coefficients are not reported in this table; these may be obtained from the author. Eurobarometer did not ask about respondent's satisfaction with democracy in 2008; therefore, for the primary regression, I constructed 2008 satisfaction values for the Eurobarometer countries by averaging the 2007 and 2009 values. To ensure robustness of my findings, I replicate the original regression, excluding these 2008 Eurobarometer countries, and the relationship retains significance and substantive meaning when these observations are excluded. Significance levels in all tables are denoted by the following: *p = 0.1. **p = 0.05. ***p = 0.01.

Robustness tests of random effects model of democratic satisfaction of Internet penetration at the country level, 2004 to 2008

	Regression excluding Region Dummies	Regression excluding 2008 Eurobarometer Countries	Regression excluding Human Development Index	Regression excluding Press Freedom Index	Regression excluding Governmental Effectiveness
Internet Penetration Rate	−.59 (.27) ($p \leq .03$)	−.62 (.28) ($p \leq .03$)	−.56 (.25) ($p \leq .02$)	−.58 (.28) ($p \leq .04$)	−.59 (.25) ($p \leq .02$)
Voice and Accountability	.21 (.17) ($p \leq .21$)	.08 (.17) ($p \leq .66$)	.12 (.17) ($p \leq .47$)	−.26 (.16) ($p \leq .1$)	.24 (.14) ($p \leq .09$)
Interaction of Internet Penetration Rate and Voice and Accountability	1.6 (.72) ($p \leq .03$)	.92 (.32) ($p \leq .004$)	.8 (.3) ($p \leq .007$)	.73 (.33) ($p \leq .006$)	.86 (.3) ($p \leq .004$)
Human Development Index	−.05 (.15) ($p \leq .76$)	.56 (.25) ($p \leq .02$)		−.81 (.33) ($p \leq .02$)	.64 (.22) ($p \leq .005$)
Press Freedom Index	−.1 (.09) ($p \leq .23$)	−.04 (.09) ($p \leq .61$)	−.1 (.08) ($p \leq .22$)		−.03 (.08) ($p \leq .69$)
Governmental Effectiveness	.48 (.13) ($p \leq .001$)	.2 (.13) ($p \leq .13$)	.34 (.12) ($p \leq .006$)	.66 (.13) ($p \leq .001$)	
Intercept	.44	.21	.33	.4	.05
Overall *r*-squared	41%	55%	11%	41%	56%
Number of Observations	247	223	250	247	247
Number of Countries	73	73	74	73	73

Note. Dependent variable is the percentage of citizens that are fairly or highly satisfied with their nation's quality of democracy. Standard errors are reported in parentheses.

Effect of Internet Use: The Country Level 77

TABLE A 4.3. Random effects regression of democratic satisfaction on Internet penetration, with Freedom House's Civil Liberties Index

	Slope	Standard Error	95% CI	p-value
Internet Penetration Rate 0–1 range, mean = 0.33, sd = 0.19)	0.23	0.13	[–0.01, 0.48]	≤0.07*
FH Civil Liberties Index (1–7 range, mean = 0.67, sd = 0.22)	0.03	0.03	[–0.02, 0.08]	≤0.3
Interaction of Internet Penetration Rate and FH Civil Liberties Index (0–1 range, mean = 0.26, sd = 0.25)	–0.12	0.07	[–0.26, 0.02]	≤0.09*
Human Development Index (0–1 range, mean = 0.8, sd = 0.14)	0.5	0.24	[0.04, 0.96]	≤0.04**
Press Freedom Index (0–1 range, mean = 0.67, sd = 0.18)	0.01	0.09	[–0.16, 0.18]	≤0.9
Governmental Effectiveness (0–1 range, mean = 0.63, sd = 0.23)	0.38	0.12	[0.16, 0.62]	≤0.001**
Intercept	–0.2			
Number of observations: 246				
Number of countries: 73				
Average number of observations per country: 3.4				
Adjusted r-squared overall: 48%				

Note. Dependent variable is the percentage of citizens that are fairly or highly satisfied with their nation's quality of democracy, scored to a continuous 0–1 range. It has a mean of 0.49 and a standard deviation of 0.19. For brevity's sake, the region-dummy coefficients are not reported in this table; these may be obtained from the author.

TABLE A 4.4. Random effects regression of democratic satisfaction, on Internet penetration, with Freedom House's Political Rights Index

	Slope	Standard Error	95% CI	p-value
Internet Penetration Rate 0–1 range, mean = 0.33, sd = 0.19)	0.21	0.13	[−0.04, 0.46]	≤0.1*
FH Political Rights Index (1–7 range, mean = 0.67, sd = 0.22)	0.02	0.02	[−0.02, 0.05]	≤0.32
Interaction of Internet Penetration Rate and FH Political Rights Index (0–1 range, mean = 0.26, sd = 0.25)	−0.1	0.07	[−0.23, 0.03]	≤0.13
Human Development Index (0–1 range, mean = 0.8, sd = 0.14)	0.46	0.23	[0.01, 0.92]	≤0.05**
Press Freedom Index (0–1 range, mean = 0.67, sd = 0.18)	−0.001	0.09	[−0.17, 0.17]	≤0.98
Governmental Effectiveness (0–1 range, mean = 0.63, sd = 0.23)	0.39	0.12	[0.16, 0.62]	0.001***
Intercept	−0.15			
Number of observations: 246 Number of countries: 73 Average number of observations per country: 3.4 Adjusted r-squared overall: 48%				

Note. Dependent variable is the percentage of citizens that are fairly or highly satisfied with their nation's quality of democracy, scored to a continuous 0–1 range. It has a mean of 0.49 and a standard deviation of 0.19. For brevity's sake, the region-dummy coefficients are not reported in this table; these may be obtained from the author.

Appendix 4.2. Sources and Surveys Used to Build Dependent Variable of Democratic Satisfaction

Survey	Reference	Question Wording	Countries
East Asian Barometer	National Taiwan University, Department of Political Science. Retrieved from: http://www .jdsurvey.net/eab/ EABContact.jsp	Please tell me how satisfied or unsatisfied you are with the following aspect of your life: the democratic system.	Indonesia Mongolia Philippines Singapore Taiwan Thailand Vietnam
Eurobarometer (Standard and Eastern and Central European)	European Commission (http://europa .eu.int/comm/ public_opinion/).	On the whole are you very satisfied, fairly satisfied, not very satisfied, or not at all satisfied with the way democracy works in (our country)?	Austria Belgium Bulgaria Cyprus Czech Republic Denmark Estonia Finland France Germany Greece Hungary Ireland Italy Latvia Lithuania Luxembourg Malta Netherlands Poland Portugal Romania Slovakia Slovenia Spain Sweden Turkey United Kingdom

Survey	Reference	Question Wording	Countries
Latinobarometer	Latinobarometro Corporation. Retrieved from: http://www .latinobarometro .org/latino/ LATDatos.jsp	In general would you say that you are very satisfied, fairly satisfied, not very satisfied, or not at all satisfied with the way democracy works in (nation)?	Argentina Bolivia Brazil Chile Colombia Costa Rica Ecuador El Salvador Guatemala Honduras Mexico Nicaragua Paraguay Peru Uruguay Venezuela
Afrobarometer	Afrobarometer. Retrieved from: www. afrobarometer .org	Overall, how satisfied are you with the way democracy works in (your country)?	Benin Botswana Burkina Faso Cape Verde Côte d'Ivoire Ghana Kenya Lesotho Liberia Madagascar Malawi Mali Mozambique Namibia Nigeria Senegal South Africa Tanzania Uganda Zambia Zimbabwe

CHAPTER 5

Determining the Effect of Internet Use on Democratic (Dis)Satisfaction

The Individual Level

ALTHOUGH THE FINDINGS uncovered by the previous chapter's country-level regression substantiate the Internet's significant and interactive effect on democratic satisfaction, as with any aggregate data analysis, there is the risk of committing an ecological fallacy. This is an error of inference caused by assuming that an observed association between aggregate-level variables also exists at the individual level. In this chapter, I therefore test the effect of the Internet on democratic (dis)satisfaction at the individual level.

The most common examples of ecological fallacies arise in the fields of health and epidemiological studies, in which aggregate findings are inappropriately applied to individuals. In one example, if comparative data reveal a correlation between nations' average dietary fat intake and higher rates of breast cancer, one might automatically conclude that women who consume diets higher in fat are more predisposed to developing breast cancer. However, without further research that might be unwise, because it may be the case that there are confounding factors that drive both a nation's incidence of breast cancer and fat intake (Pearce 2000). Thus, in general, researchers must be circumspect in applying aggregate-level relationships to individuals.

To address this concern, it is necessary to test whether the relationship shared by Internet penetration and democratic satisfaction holds when the unit of analysis shifts to the individual. By means of triangulation, if the same relationship is revealed at multiple levels of analysis and employing different models, this provides a robust empirical foundation for testing the Internet's effects.

In this chapter, the primary individual-level regression employs cross-sectional survey data that incorporates the responses of over 45,000 individuals living in forty-seven different Western European, Central and Eastern European, and Latin American countries.[1] Across these countries, Internet penetration in 2005 ranges from a low of 3 percent of Nicaraguans using the Internet to a high of 81 percent of the Swedish population using it. The average level of Internet penetration across these nations is 35 percent, with a standard deviation of 23 percent.

Since it is likely that there are important country-level factors that influence the individual-level relationship shared by Internet use and democratic satisfaction, in this chapter I employ a multiple-level (i.e., hierarchical) regression model. Multiple-level models have the advantage of enabling an individual-level analysis while simultaneously accounting for systematic variation at the country level that is difficult to identify or difficult to control.

In the following sections, I introduce the variables used in this analysis. I then discuss the advantages of a multi-level (i.e., hierarchical) model and report the results of this primary regression. Before concluding, I conduct an additional test of the relationship shared by Internet use and democratic (dis)satisfaction by employing cross-sectional data from surveys conducted before and after the Internet became widely available. This enables the construction of a two-stage auxiliary instrumental variable predicting an individual's likelihood of Internet use.

The advantage of this model is that it allows researchers to estimate a "panel" relationship when only successive cross-sectional surveys are available, thus approximating a time-series cross-sectional analysis. As discussed in the previous chapter, such an analysis is considered more dynamic and thus more rigorous than a test based on data from only a single snapshot in time. Finally, this additional test also further broadens the empirical foundation substantiating the Internet's effect on democratic (dis)satisfaction.

The Variables

In building this model, it is necessary to include a number of demographic factors that are plausibly correlated with both democratic satisfaction and one's likelihood of using the Internet. First, the model controls for education level, since this is correlated both with one's likelihood of using the Internet as well as the type of information and criteria that an individual draws upon to evaluate their governments. The model also controls for the respondent's sex and age—since early Internet users tend to be male and younger than the general population. It is also likely that young people hold particular attitudes toward their democracy due to their stage in life. As for gender, in many of these countries men and women still face markedly different circumstances and access to resources, which likely influences both their access to the Internet and their political evaluations. Finally, to account for traditional media usage, the analysis includes variables representing how often the respondent reads the newspaper and watches news on the television.

It is important to note that these surveys do not include objective measures of household income as has increasingly become the norm for international surveys. In recent years, scholars have questioned not only the validity and reliability of cross-national income survey measures but also their comparability, which is defined as "the extent to which an instrument remains equal in its content, structure, mode of administration, etc. and delivers results, which, given as a whole, can be interpreted meaningfully" (Holst 2003, 367). Such concerns likely contributed to the decision made by several international survey organizations to no longer include an "objective" measure of income in comparative surveys.

While the concerns motivating this decision are sound, the omission of traditional income measures is potentially problematic for social science analyses. This is because income likely plays a confounding role in many of the relationships of interest to social scientists. By declining to collect income information from survey respondents, social scientists' ability to control for the influence of income in the relationship they are testing is limited. In this case, it is feasible that an individual's income level influences both their likelihood of Internet use and their democratic satisfaction; thus, ideally, an analysis will control for the effect of income to be sure that the model is testing the direct effect of Internet use on satisfaction.

Concerns regarding doing away with traditional income measures are assuaged by two factors, however. First, education and income tend to be highly correlated, so the fact that these analyses can still include measures of a respondent's education somewhat mitigates concerns regarding the under-specification of models. Additionally, scholars have proposed alternative versions of the traditional income measure that are argued to be more consistent and comparable across borders. One such alternative, proposed by Holst (2003), is a summary index of the ownership of household goods—ranging from a color television to a car, to a house. Averaging the number of household goods each respondent owns out of the total number of items asked by each survey can serve as a proxy measure of income that is claimed to be more meaningfully comparable across borders. Accordingly,

I re-ran the original regression including this proxy income variable, which altered neither the significance nor substantive meaning of the Internet's relationship with democratic satisfaction. However, since the proxy income measure did not contribute much to the model in terms of exhibiting a significant relationship with satisfaction or explaining variation in satisfaction levels, I opted not to include it in the primary regression presented in this chapter. (For more information about this proxy, see appendix 5.1.)

Turning to the independent variable *Internet use*, both the Latinobarometer and Eurobarometer surveys include questions pertaining to personal Internet use. Unfortunately, however, neither the Afrobarometer nor the East-Asian barometer included questions pertaining to personal Internet use, making those studies ineligible for inclusion in the individual-level analysis. (For more information about the construction of the personal Internet use variable, see appendix 5.2.) Additionally, I also include an *Interaction* variable of self-reported Internet use and the quality of democracy (VA) in the respondent's home country, which allows the direction of the Internet's effect to vary according to the strength of available democratic practices as the theory predicts.

Lastly, the dependent variable *Democratic Satisfaction* is an ordinal variable derived from respondents' answer to the question of how satisfied they are, in general, with the way that democracy functions in their country. The possible response options include: Very satisfied, Fairly satisfied, Not very satisfied, or Not at all satisfied. (Additional response options of Don't Know and No Answer are treated as null cells and are thus excluded from the analysis.)

The Model

This analysis employs an OLS multi-level model as the primary test of the interactive effect of Internet use on democratic satisfaction. Multi-level models enable the model to test the effect of Internet use at the individual level, while also accounting for and controlling the country-level factors that likely influence this relationship. Essentially, there are factors both within and across countries that influence the Internet's effect on satisfaction. Thus, by using a multi-level model it is possible to separate and estimate the variance both within and across these countries. This means that the model holds various country-level factors constant, enabling the analysis to focus specifically on the effect of the Internet on the individual citizens within these countries.

At the individual level, using the Internet is significantly correlated with democratic satisfaction, reaching the .01 significance level. Moreover, as predicted by Hypothesis 1 (that Internet use will increase satisfaction with democracy in nations boasting high-functioning democracies but depress satisfaction in nations with poor democratic practices), the quality of national democratic practices that a citizen enjoys conditions the direction of the Internet's effect on democratic satisfaction. In fact, the threshold point at which Internet users become more dissatisfied than non-users mirrors that revealed by the aggregate-level regression in chapter 4. Specifically, the direction of the Internet's effect on democratic satisfaction shifts from negative to positive in nations that are ranked around the 70th percentile in terms of strength of democratic practices. Above this threshold, Internet users are more satisfied than non-users living in the same countries; however, below this threshold, Internet users become increasingly more dissatisfied than non-Internet users living in the same country (see figure 5.1).

Additionally, error bars in figure 5.1 represent the 95 percent confidence intervals derived from an estimation of the average marginal effects of the interaction term coefficients. These error bars illustrate the points at which we see clear and significant differential effects of being an Internet user in countries with various levels of strength of democratic practices. Other than the threshold point where the direction of the effect switches from negative to positive, there are consistently clear and significant differential effects of Internet use on democratic satisfaction across the range of countries included in this analysis. Whereas in a country ranked at the 40th percentile in terms of strength of democratic practices, Internet use decreases satisfaction by an average of 5 percentage points; on the other end of the spectrum, Internet use increases democratic satisfaction by an average of 4 percentage points in countries ranked in the 99th percentile.

It is worth noting that the effect of Internet use within each country is relatively moderate in terms of the substantive size of the effect. In other words, relative to non-users, the size of the marginal effect of Internet use on democratic satisfaction depresses satisfaction by 9 percentage points in countries ranked on the lowest end of this scale and increases satisfaction by 4 percentage points in countries with the strongest democratic practices. However, this remains a meaningful, albeit moderate, effect—one would be hard pressed to find a campaign manager or strategic communication specialist who would discount the import of even a 4-percentage-point shift in public opinion. Moreover, looking at these findings through a different lens,

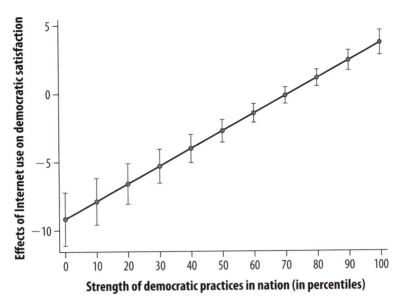

FIGURE 5.1 Average Marginal Effects of Internet Use on Democratic Satisfaction (with 95% Confidence Intervals)

it is also worth noting the remarkable variability in the size and direction of the Internet's effect on satisfaction contingent on strength of national democratic practices—a 13-percentage-point difference in satisfaction between countries ranked at the lowest end of the scale and those ranked at the highest end. Thus, as the number of Internet users across the globe continues to expand, the political implications of this shift in public opinion and the incentives for officials to heed that shift will have meaningful and tangible political consequences.

In summary, these results corroborate the relationship uncovered at the country-level and further substantiate the contingent effect of the Internet on democratic satisfaction hypothesized by the mirror-holding and window-opening functions. While using the Internet in Denmark, whose strength of democratic practices is ranked in the 99th percentile, enhances satisfaction by nearly 4 percentage points, Internet use in Venezuela, ranked in the 29th percentile, depresses satisfaction with how democracy functions in that nation by more than 5 percentage points. (See table A5.1. Note that all regression tables in this chapter are included in appendix 5.3.)

The results of the primary individual level regression support and strengthen the interactive effect of the Internet on democratic satisfaction substantiated in the previous chapter. However, since this regression is based on cross-sectional survey data from a single slice in time, there are potentially a number of methodological concerns with such an analysis. First, the model may suffer from misspecification (i.e., the correlation between Internet use and satisfaction is not a result of a direct causal relationship, but rather of their relation to another omitted variable). It is also possible that, contrary to my theory, causality runs in the opposite direction, with democratic (dis) satisfaction driving Internet use. Finally, it is also possible that Internet use and democratic satisfaction share an endogenous relationship, which would be the case if Internet use and democratic satisfaction exert a reciprocal influence on one another. Endogeneity is problematic for an OLS regression because the regression coefficient becomes biased and inconsistent, making it difficult to accurately gauge the independent and direct influence of Internet use on democratic satisfaction.

Panel data, in which the same individuals are interviewed about their democratic satisfaction before and after their introduction to the Internet, would be ideal for addressing these concerns. Unfortunately, to my knowledge, no such survey data yet exist at the individual level. A second-best approach is to build an instrumental variable predicting an individual's likelihood of accessing the Internet. By employing cross-sectional data from surveys conducted before and after the Internet became widely available, I thus construct a two-stage auxiliary instrumental variable (Franklin 1989) predicting an individual's likelihood of Internet use. This enables researchers to estimate a "panel" relationship when only successive cross-sectional surveys are available—as is the case with the Globalbarometer surveys.

Essentially, this allows the analysis to use variables strongly correlated with Internet use, once the Internet became widely available, to predict a given individual's likelihood of using the Internet in years *before* the Internet was available. If this predictor variable exhibits a distinct relationship with democratic satisfaction before and after the Internet becomes widely available, then it can be reasonably concluded that Internet use is driving democratic (dis)satisfaction, rather than the inverse.

This would also assuage misspecification concerns because a potentially omitted influence would plausibly be consistent across both 1997 and 2005, and therefore the effect of predicted Internet use and democratic satisfaction would remain consistent across these two time periods. However, if the relationship between predicted Internet use and satisfaction differs between these two time periods, then it can be reasonably concluded that it is the growth of Internet use that drove changes in democratic satisfaction as opposed to some omitted influence.

Fortunately, the longevity of the Eurobarometer and Latinobarometer series lends these surveys nicely to an analysis employing a two-stage auxiliary instrumental variable. Accordingly, to compare the effect of being a "predicted Internet user" on democratic satisfaction before and after the Internet widely came into use, I compare the effect of being a predicted Internet user on democratic satisfaction in 1997 (before the Internet was largely in use) to that of 2005 (when the Internet was widely in use). Since 1997 is the first year that the Internet was commercially available outside of the United States, it is reasonable to conclude that the vast majority of respondents living in Latin America and Europe had not used the Internet in 1997.[2] However, by 2005, Internet penetration rates reached an average of 40 percent across European countries and 20 percent in Latin America.

These two Globalbarometer surveys fulfill two additional criteria important to such a two-stage analysis. First, the primary and secondary surveys each sample from the same population. And, second, there is neither an extended lapse in time nor a monumental exogenous shock (that is, a major event) separating these two surveys.

In building this auxiliary variable, I employ three variables that are highly predictive of an individual's likelihood of using the Internet in 2005: owning a computer, having landline telephone service at home, and living in a large community. Each is significantly correlated with Internet use in 2005. Moreover, there is sound theoretical justification for using these factors to generate each individual's predicted likelihood of using the Internet.

First, owning a computer is logically correlated with one's propensity to use the Internet, not only because it provides the technological capacity to access the Internet but also the computer skills and know-how to navigate the Internet. Having telephone service in the home is also predictive of Internet use because Internet service originally reached homes through telephone lines via ISDN (integrated services digital network). Finally, including the size of the community that each individual lives in is predictive of Internet use, since the technological infrastructure that permits Internet access tends to diffuse first to large urban areas. (See table A5.2 for results of regression to build instrument for the 2SLS Analysis.)

After regressing these factors on self-reported Internet use in 2005, I can use the derived parameters to generate predicted-Internet-use values for each of the 1997 and 2005 survey respondents. If the effect of predicted

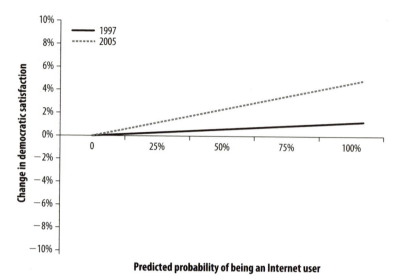

FIGURE 5.2 Effect of Increased Likelihood of Using the Internet on Democratic Satisfaction in Luxembourg, 1997 versus 2005

probability of using the Internet on democratic satisfaction is different in 2005 (when the Internet was available in these countries) than in 1997 (before the Internet was broadly available), this will yield yet another piece of evidence supporting the direct causal influence of Internet use on democratic satisfaction. If the Internet has a direct and independent influence on satisfaction, there should be a statistically significant difference in the effect of being a predicted Internet user on democratic satisfaction across these two time periods.

RESULTS

To determine if the likelihood of being a predicted Internet user produces a distinct effect on democratic satisfaction in 2005, when the Internet was widely in use, compared to 1997, when the Internet had only just become commercially available, I regressed predicted Internet use on satisfaction across both time periods, with a dummy variable and interaction term representing the year 2005. The results of this regression confirm that predicted Internet use exerts a substantially and significantly different effect on satisfaction in 2005 relative to 1997 (see table A5.3).

Since this model includes a triple interaction term, which can be difficult to interpret, the discussion of the substantive meaning of these findings compares the effect of predicted Internet use in 1997 and 2005 in specific

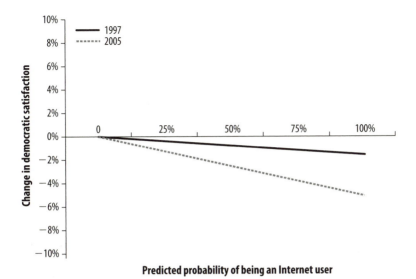

FIGURE 5.3 Effect of Increased Likelihood of Using the Internet on Democratic Satisfaction in Bolivia, 1997 versus 2005

countries on each side of the spectrum in terms of strength of democratic practices. Specifically, in Luxembourg (whose strength of democratic practices is ranked in the 95th percentile) the effect of moving from having 0 percent likelihood of using the Internet to 100 percent likelihood of using the Internet in 1997 had little discernible effect on one's level of democratic satisfaction—increasing satisfaction by only 1 percentage point. However, in 2005, predicted Internet users' level of democratic satisfaction in Luxembourg is nearly 5 percentage points greater than that of their counterparts with no predicted likelihood of using the Internet (see figure 5.2).

On the other hand, in Bolivia, whose strength of democratic practices is ranked on the other end of the spectrum (the 40th percentile), the effect of moving from 0 percent likelihood of using the Internet to 100 percent likelihood also exerts a distinct effect across the two periods. In 1997 the effect of moving along the spectrum of predicted Internet use exerted marginal effect on democratic satisfaction (~ 1 percentage point). However, not only did the effect of being a predicted Internet user significantly differ in 2005 compared to 1997, but it markedly decreased one's democratic satisfaction, the predicted effect of Internet use in a nation with weak democratic practices (see figure 5.3).

In sum, while the interactive relationship shared by predicted Internet use and satisfaction attained statistical significance in 2005 (p-value = .01), this relationship failed to approach significance in 1997. Moreover, predicted Internet use shared a significant and interactive relationship with democratic satisfaction in 2005, which mirrored the size and strength of the relationship shared by actual Internet use and satisfaction uncovered by the primary multi-level cross-sectional regression. Most importantly, the 2005 relationship shared by predicted Internet use and democratic satisfaction was significantly and substantively distinct from that in 1997. This mitigates endogeneity and misspecification concerns and sets the causal arrow firmly in place by revealing that Internet use does exert a direct and independent influence on democratic satisfaction.

Conclusion

The results of an OLS multi-level regression of cross-sectional survey data further demonstrate the Internet's conditional influence on democratic satisfaction (p-value $\leq .01$). Whereas in top-performing democracies individuals that use the Internet are more satisfied with their nation's democracy when compared to non-users, in a nation with weak democratic practices using the Internet depresses an individual's democratic satisfaction relative to their non-Internet-using counterparts.

I undertook an additional regression employing a two-stage auxiliary instrumental variable to address the endogeneity and misspecification concerns that tend to accompany cross-sectional analyses. Consistent with my hypothesis, this instrumental variable exerted a significantly (p-value $\leq .01$) and substantively distinct influence on democratic satisfaction in 2005 (when individuals were using the Internet) compared to 1997 (when the Internet was not widely in use). In combination, these results offer clear and consistent evidence that the Internet is, in fact, exerting the direct and causal influence on democratic satisfaction, conditioned by the actual strength of democratic practices available in a country.

Appendix 5.1. The Proxy Income Variable

To explore the validity of the proxy income variable proposed by Holst (2003), I tested its correlation against the two subjective income questions included by the Latinobarometer survey. The first question asked respondents to "imagine a 10-step ladder, where in '1' stand the poorest people and in '10' stand the richest people. Where would you stand?" The second question asked the interviewer to evaluate the respondents' socioeconomic status based on the "quality of housing, quality of furniture, and respondent's looks." The level of correlation revealed between the proxy income measure and each of the subjective income measures (.41 and .51, respectively) was higher than the correlation shared by the two subjective measures themselves (.34).

Appendix 5.2. The Internet Use Variable

While the Latinobarometer did include a question directly asking individuals about the nature of their Internet use (i.e., "No matter where you have access to the Internet, what do you frequently use the Internet for?"—with the answer "Not applicable" indicating non-users), the Eurobarometer did not include a direct measure of Internet use. However, since my theory predicts an interactive relationship between Internet use and satisfaction contingent on the strength of democratic practices in a nation, it is important that the countries included in the individual-level analysis range widely across the spectrum of possible democratic performance. Excluding the European countries from this analysis would leave only those countries ranked in the bottom quartiles of democratic performance and therefore only those that fall below the threshold identified by the country-level regression in which the Internet's effect moves from negative to positive.

In order to accommodate the European countries, I derived a proxy measurement for Internet use from two questions asked in the Eurobarometer survey: (1) "When you are looking for information about the European Union, its policies, its institutions, which of the following sources do you use?" and (2) "Which of the following (household) goods do you have?" Anyone who answered "Internet" to either or both of these questions was recorded as an Internet user, with the remainder identified as non-users.

To test the accuracy of this proxy, the percentage of Internet users in each nation predicted by this measure is compared to the official percentage of Internet users in each nation reported by the International Telecommunication Union (ITU). The average difference between these two measures is 8 percentage points, with a standard deviation of 5.4. This suggests that the proxy variable is a reasonably accurate measure of actual Internet users. However, to ensure that my analysis includes a reasonably highly accurate proxy of Internet use, I ran multiple regressions in which I included different sub-sets of users to test the robustness.

Specifically, I replicated this regression with a number of different combinations of European nations, including a regression with all of the European countries included, a regression with no European countries included, and a regression with those European countries in which the proxy measurement fell within 5 percentage points of the actual percentage of Internet users in that nation. In each of these regressions, the results are comparable to those of the primary regression in both substantive and significance terms. In this chapter, I opted to include the results of the analysis which included all of the nations.

Appendix 5.3. Regression Results for Chapter 5

TABLE A 5.1.   Multilevel regression of democratic satisfaction on Internet use at the individual level

	Slope	Standard Error	95% CI	p-value
Internet Use (0–1 binary, mean = 0.37, sd = 0.48)	−0.09	0.01	[−0.11, −0.07]	≤0.001***
Voice and Accountability (0–1 range, mean = 0.67, sd = 0.22)	0.27	0.07	[0.14, 0.4]	≤0.001***
Interaction of Internet Access and Voice and Accountability (0–1 range, mean = 0.27, sd = 0.38)	0.13	0.01	[0.1, 0.15]	≤0.001***
Education (0–1 range, mean = 0.52, sd = 0.3)	0.003	0.006	[−0.007, 0.02]	≤0.49
Age (0–1 range, mean = 0.45, sd = 0.33)	−0.02	0.005	[−0.02, −0.004]	≤0.001***
Male (0–1 binary, mean = 0.48, sd = 0.49)	0.006	0.003	[0.001, 0.01]	≤0.01***
Newspaper (0–1 range, mean = 0.41, sd = 0.41)	0.02	0.004	[0.02, 0.03]	≤0.001***
Television News (0–1 range, mean = 0.72, sd = 0.34)	0.006	0.004	[−0.002, 0.01]	≤0.18
Intercept	0.24	0.05	[0.15, 0.34]	≤0.001***

Country-Level Parameters	Estimate	Standard Error	95% CI
Estimated Standard Deviation in Intercept	0.09	0.01	[0.07, 0.12]
Estimated Standard Deviation in Error Term (i.e., Variability)	0.26	0.001	[0.26, 0.264]

Likelihood-Ratio Test Comparing Multiple-Level Model to OLS Model:
chibar2(01) = 4,851 Prob ≥ chibar2 = 0.00***

Number of Observations: 45,223
Number of Countries: 47
Average Number of Observations
  per Country: 962

Note. Dependent variable is satisfaction with one's democracy, scored to a discrete 0–1 range. 1 denotes that the individual is very satisfied, while 0 is assigned to individuals that report being very unsatisfied. Intermediate categories include fairly satisfied (0.66) and fairly unsatisfied (0.33). This variable has a mean of 0.45 and a standard deviation of 0.29.

TABLE A 5.2.   Instrument for two-stage auxiliary instrumental variable of predicted Internet use

	Slope	Standard Error	95% CI	p-value
Phone Ownership (0–1 binary, mean = 0.62, sd = 0.49)	0.06	0.004	[0.05, 0.07]	≤0.001***
Computer Ownership (0–1 binary, mean = 0.37, sd = 0.48)	0.6	0.005	[0.59, 0.61]	≤0.001***
Size of Community (0–1 range, mean = 0.54, sd = 0.4)	0.07	0.004	[0.09, 0.1]	≤0.001***
Intercept	0.09	0.004	[0.09, 0.1]	
Number of Observations: 36,102 Adjusted r-squared: 38%				

Note. Dependent variable is being an Internet user in 2005 (0–1 binary, mean = 0.39, sd = 0.49).

TABLE A 5.3. Individual-level regression of predicted Internet use and democratic satisfaction in 1997 and 2005

	Slope	Standard Error	95% CI	p-value
2005 Predicted Internet User (0–1 range, mean = 0.2, sd = 0.29)	−0.11	0.03	[−0.16, −0.05]	≤0.001***
2005 Voice and Accountability (0–1 range, mean = 0.35, sd = 0.39)	−0.03	0.03	[−0.08, 0.02]	≤0.23
2005 Predicted Internet User × Voice and Accountability (0–1 range, mean = 0.15, sd = 0.25)	0.16	0.04	[0.08, 0.24]	≤0.001***
Year 2005 (0–1 binary, mean = 0.5, sd = 0.5)	−0.03	0.02	[−0.05, 0.01]	≤0.11
1997 Predicted Internet User × Voice and Accountability (0–1 range, mean = 0.27, sd = 0.27)	0.03	0.04	[−0.06, 0.1]	≤0.54
1997 Predicted Internet User (0–1 binary, mean = 0.34, sd = 0.29)	−0.02	0.03	[−0.07, 0.093]	≤0.4
1997 Voice and Accountability (0–1 range, mean = 0.72, sd = 0.23)	0.04	0.03	[−0.01, 0.08]	≤0.16
Education (0–1 range, mean = 0.52, sd = 0.28)	0.007	0.006	[−0.004, 0.02]	≤0.2
Age (0–1 range, mean = 0.44, sd = 0.33)	0.002	0.004	[−0.006, 0.01]	≤0.68
Male (0–1 binary, mean = 0.48, sd = 0.5)	0.004	0.002	[−0.0005, 0.009]	≤0.08*
Newspaper (0–1 range, mean = 0.5, sd = 0.39)	0.02	0.004	[0.01, 0.023]	≤0.001*
Television News (0–1 range, mean = 0.7, sd = 0.34)	0.002	0.004	[−0.006, 0.01]	≤0.38
Intercept	0.48	0.02	[0.44, 0.52]	≤0.001***
Number of cases: 49,309 Adjusted r-squared: 14%				

Note. Dependent variable is satisfaction with one's democracy, scored to a discrete 0–1 range. 1 denotes that the individual is very satisfied, while 0 is assigned to individuals that report being very unsatisfied. Intermediate categories include fairly satisfied (0.66) and fairly unsatisfied (0.33). This variable has a mean of 0.46 and a standard deviation of 0.29. For the sake of brevity, country dummy coefficients are not reported; these results may be obtained from the author.

CHAPTER 6

At the Internet Café
A Test for Democratic Satisfaction in Bosnia and Herzegovina

COUNTRY-LEVEL AND INDIVIDUAL-LEVEL analyses independently and mutually substantiate the Internet's conditional effect on democratic satisfaction: whereas the Internet strengthens satisfaction in robust democracies, Internet access depresses satisfaction among users living in nations with weak democratic practices. However, in addition a randomized experiment described in this chapter provides a direct test of the causal relationship shared by Internet use and democratic (dis)satisfaction. This is an important contribution to the study of the political effects of Internet use, since such direct tests of causality are scarce in the extant literature.

This experiment also enables a broader exploration of related evaluations and democratic attitudes that are integral to the cost-benefit calculus of political behavior and that may, in some instances, motivate individuals to act and organize to effect political change. These include whether the Internet provides information that enables users to make more "accurate" evaluations of the quality of democratic practices in their own country, the level of trust individuals have in their government, and the terms through which individuals conceptualize democracy.

In addition, while at first glance the finding that the Internet encourages more critical evaluations of poorly performing governments may seem to bode well for the Internet as a positive force for democracy and democratization, upon further reflection it is conceivable that dissatisfaction could produce two very divergent reactions in disgruntled Internet users. On the one hand, dissatisfied citizens may be rallied to lobby their governments for higher standards of democratic practices, a potential boon to the long-term development of democracy in these nations. On the other hand, dissatisfaction might encourage citizens to take an increasingly dim view of democracy in general, perhaps even questioning its appropriateness as the system of governance for their own country. This could be problematic for the process of democratization, particularly considering previous research that has shown that an individual's evaluation of democracy in practice is the single biggest predictor of their support for democratic norms in general (Evans & Whitefield 1995).

As a further test of my hypothesis, I conducted a field experiment in Zenica, the fourth-largest city in the nation of Bosnia and Herzegovina, between July and October of 2007. In this randomized experiment, I arranged for participants to receive free Internet use in the town's local Internet café for a period of two months. Using pretest and posttest questionnaires, I tested the effect of Internet exposure on participants' satisfaction with how democracy functions in Bosnia and Herzegovina, their evaluations of the quality of Bosnian democracy, and their beliefs regarding what constitutes good democratic governance.

Why a Field Experiment?

Field experiments offer many advantages to the study of political communication, complementing large-n quantitative analyses of survey data by providing a more substantial empirical foundation for causal claims of media effects. Large-n statistical analyses of survey data tend to be plagued by weak internal validity. That is, survey instruments do not necessarily always measure what they purport to measure. They also tend to suffer from weak causal inference. For example, can one be reasonably confident that it is Internet use that drives (dis)satisfaction? Or, is the reverse direction of causation more feasible?

While experiments can be handicapped by weak external validity—that is, behavior in a laboratory doesn't always generalize to the real world—they allow the researcher to precisely control the variables of interest, thereby maximizing internal validity. Through random assignment and careful control over the temporal ordering of variables, experiments also offer the strongest test possible for causality. Finally, by doing the experiment in the field—on actual citizens recruited from the community at large who are using the Internet as they naturally would, rather than drawing exclusively from college undergraduate populations—it is possible to also increase external validity (at least relative to laboratory experiments). Combining statistical analyses of survey data with field experiments, therefore, provides a strong empirical foundation for understanding the nature of the Internet's influence on evaluations and democratic attitudes.

While laboratory experiments contributed to many of the greatest advances in political communication research since the field's renaissance began in the 1970s—particularly in identifying and testing the effects of framing, priming, campaign negativity, and agenda-setting—field experiments remain a very underutilized method in this discipline. This is likely for very pragmatic reasons: field experiments are both difficult and costly to execute well. However, as information and communication technologies (ICT) continue to diffuse rapidly throughout the globe—often into regions that were previously nearly devoid of such capabilities—opportunities such as the following abound to explore how these technologies interact with and influence political attitudes, behaviors, and outcomes.

Bosnia and Herzegovina

Exacerbated by the loss of nearly 200,000 lives, the internal displacement of nearly one million residents, and the out-migration of more than another million residents, the harsh repercussions of the 1992–1995 war are still evident in Bosnia's continuing economic and social woes. For example, after the war, GDP plummeted by 80 percent, and official unemployment rates still stood at about 29 percent in 2007, with one-quarter of the population reported to live below the poverty line (Central Intelligence Agency 2008). In Zenica, located about seventy kilometers north of the capital city of Sarajevo, the steel industry had a particularly hard time transitioning to economic liberalization. As a consequence, in 2007 the town suffered one of the worst unemployment rates and poverty rates of any non-rural area in the nation.

Bosnia's political domain was not faring much better. In order to appease the Serb, Croat, and Bosniak factions, the 1995 Dayton Peace Accord put into place a highly complicated and convoluted governing structure. For example, at the federal level, the presidential office is shared by three concurrent members—a Serb, a Bosniak, and a Croat—who are elected by popular election every four years and rotate the lead position of chairman every eight months. The nation's legislature is bicameral, composed of the House of Representatives (elected for four-year terms by popular vote on the basis of proportional representation) and the House of Peoples (chosen by the legislatures of the two entities to serve four-year terms). Ultimately, however, the nation's highest political authority was the High Representative in Bosnia and Herzegovina. The Dayton Accord created the Office of the High Representative (OHR), which it charged with overseeing the implementation of the civilian aspects of the Accord in representation of the international community. Accordingly, in recent years the OHR "has dismissed elected officials, including the president of the Serb Republic in 1999, and banned political parties that are opposed to the Dayton Peace Accords" (Freedom House 2003).

Not surprisingly—although the majority of the nation's highest government officials are elected by popular vote, and although the U.S. State Department lists the government of Bosnia and Herzegovina as a "parliamentary democracy"—many international organizations questioned the extent of real democratic practices extant in Bosnia as of 2007. The problems with the present system are manifold. In brief, the supreme authority of the Office of the High Representative suggests that the nation functions more as a protectorate than a democracy. In addition, corruption continued to run rampant among government officials, calling into question the transparency of the political process and the accountability of its elected officials. The 2002 elections also witnessed a resurgence of the nationalist parties, widely considered a setback to the democratic process due to their factionalist and combative platforms (Freedom House 2003). Moreover, a 2007 U.S. State Department country report revealed that the government's human rights record remains poor, citing continued police abuse of detainees, harassment of newspersons by political parties and authorities, manipulation of the judiciary, and religious discrimination.

Finally, there is worry that the greatest long-term threat to democratization in Bosnia is the looming "temptation of authoritarianism," which is defined as the inherited notion that public policy is best formulated by elites outside of the political process: "At the heart of the Bosnian governance problem . . . lies the lack of engagement by Bosnian citizens and interest groups in the practice of government. . . . Just as a company without the interest of an owner will not use its assets wisely, public institutions which are not subject to constant pressure from citizens exerted through the democratic process will not respond to the needs of the public effectively" (European Stability Initiative 2004).

According to United Nation's International Telecommunications Union (ITU) agency reports, Internet penetration in Bosnia had reached nearly 27 percent of the population in 2007. The primary type of Internet connection remained the Integrated Services Digital Network (ISDN), which uses traditional telephone lines. However, as of 2007, 8 percent of the total number of Internet subscribers in Bosnia utilized the more advanced broadband technology (ITU 2008). In addition, there are no formal restrictions on Internet use or content at the government level.

Accordingly, Bosnia and Herzegovina provided a good fit for this experiment because it met the following parameters. First, the quality of Bosnia's democratic performance was low enough (i.e., far enough below the threshold identified in previous analyses where the effect of Internet use on satisfaction turns negative) to expect that Internet use will demonstrably depress satisfaction. Second, the technological infrastructure for Internet use was in place, although a sizeable number of the population could not afford to use the Internet. This is essential, due to my desire to recruit subjects with minimal to no previous experience on the Internet, so that a two-month exposure to the Internet constitutes a reasonably large treatment condition over the baseline.

PROCEDURE

With the aid of a research assistant, I recruited subjects by airing radio commercials, posting fliers, stuffing mailboxes, and setting up a booth with signs in the city center. The commercials, fliers, and signs advertised free Internet hours at an Internet café in exchange for filling out surveys. Over a period of ten days we collected more than 150 names and phone numbers from interested individuals. We then used a random number generator to assign 60 individuals to the experimental group, 60 individuals to the control group, and the remainder to serve as alternates in the event that members of the experimental or control groups declined to participate.

After randomly dividing the subjects into the control and Internet (i.e., treatment) groups, my assistant and I called the participants in the control group and advised them that they had not been selected to receive two months of free Internet use but that they would be contacted again in two months and offered free time on the Internet in return for completing a survey. Next, we called the individuals randomly assigned to Internet group and asked them to meet us at the Internet café. Upon reading the consent form and indicating their consent, participants were asked to fill out pretest questionnaires. These questionnaires were relatively short and contained only one question pertaining specifically to satisfaction with democracy. In addition, the pretest contained an array of questions on other topics intended to mask the true focus of the study, including questions about Bosnian pop culture and sports. After the participants completed the pretest, we gave them a coupon booklet that entitled them to 60 hours of free Internet use at the cafe. We also offered them brief tutorials on Internet use, including how to navigate from one page to another and how to set up email accounts.

The Internet café used for the experiment was Zenica.net, located in the city center. Zenica.net was the first Internet café created in Bosnia and Herzegovina after the war, in 1998, with funding from USAID and the Soros Foundation. It has about fifteen computers, each of which used a relatively fast broadband connection by Bosnian standards (~1 MB/sec download speed). Privacy screens separated some of the computers, and there were no reported restrictions regarding the sort of websites that patrons could visit—other than the fact that a person standing behind you could potentially see your screen.

We then left the members of the Internet group to their own devices for the next two months. We made no effort to direct or influence how they used the Internet or the types of websites they chose to visit. We also did not monitor their Internet use electronically. This decision was made to minimize external validity concerns, preferring that participants use the Internet as naturally as they would in normal daily life. However, the owner of the Internet café did document the number of Internet hours that each individual used at the café. After the two-month period expired, my assistant contacted individuals in both the experimental and control groups by telephone and offered the equivalent of $3 (USD) or an additional three hours of free Internet time at the cafe to complete the post-treatment survey.

RESULTS

In line with the expectations of random assignment, the demographic characteristics of the members of the Internet and control groups did not differ in any substantively significant manner. Both groups reported, on average, completing their education one to two years into post-secondary school. The gender distribution of the Internet and control groups stood at 56 percent and 63 percent male, respectively. The average age of members in the Internet group was 29, while the control group's average age was 31. Self-reported rates of English fluency were also comparable, with each group's average English proficiency described as somewhere between being able to "speak a little" English and the ability to "hold a basic conversation" in English. Finally, the Internet group's average monthly household income was slightly higher than that of the control group; however, this was a substantively small difference, and the median value was identical across both groups.

Since the World Bank ranked Bosnia's democracy at the 51st percentile in 2007, according to my theory and the findings from my previous quantitative analyses of survey data (which indicated that the Internet's effect on satisfaction turns negative somewhere at approximately the 75th percentile), gaining Internet access should depress satisfaction with how democracy functions in Bosnia. This yields the following corollaries of Hypothesis 1:

H^{1A}: Satisfaction with how democracy functions in Bosnia should decrease among individuals' in the Internet group during their two-month period on the Internet.

H^{1B}: After the two-month period on the Internet, individuals in the Internet group should be less satisfied with how democracy functions in Bosnia than individuals in the control group.

A paired t-test indicates that, consistent with H^{1A}, the average level of democratic satisfaction among the individuals in the Internet group declined over the two-month period of Internet exposure. While the average level of democratic satisfaction originally stood at 32 percent, after the two month-period of free Internet use the Internet group's level of satisfaction dropped to 29 percent. Based on a t-test, this three-percentage-point decline is significant at the .1 level (p-value $\leq$ .08). (See table A6.1. Note that all t-test tables for this chapter are included in appendix 6.1.)

Although a search of global news publications in the archival database LexisNexis does not uncover any highly visible, exceptional national events or scandals between the administration of the pretest and posttest questionnaires (late-July to mid-October of 2007), it is still possible that events in Bosnia and Herzegovina during the same period, rather than exposure to the Internet, could have caused this decline in democratic satisfaction. Thus, I also compared the average level of satisfaction among members of the Internet group to that of members of the control group in the posttests. A two-sample t-test indicates that, consistent with H^{1B}, there is a substantive difference in the democratic satisfaction across these two groups in the direction predicted. Whereas the average satisfaction of individuals in the Internet group stood at 30 percent after spending two months on the Internet, the control group (surveyed at this same point in time) was more satisfied with Bosnian democracy, at 34 percent. This democratic satisfaction differential just misses statistical significance at .1 level. However, when non-compliers (i.e., members of the Internet group who did not use the Internet during this period and therefore were not actually exposed to the treatment) are excluded from this analysis, this differential does reach significance ($p \leq .1$), with members of the Internet group being significantly less satisfied than members of the control group. (See table A6.2 in the appendix 6.1.)

Does the Internet Encourage Individuals to Reevaluate the Quality of the National Democracy?

This question considers whether the Internet's negative influence on satisfaction is a consequence of providing information that changes users' evaluations of how democracy functions in their own country, as mirror-holding and window-opening predict. This is opposed to the possibility that the Internet's effect on satisfaction might merely be some sort of affective response such as that predicted by the theory offered by Bucy and Gregson (2001), which I refer to as a *perceived-participation theory*. According to perceived-participation, Internet use enhances satisfaction via the psychological benefits garnered from the expanded forum that the Internet provides to individuals to express their preferences to elected leaders (whether or not there is any evidence that leaders actually become any more responsive to those preferences). Although Bucy and Gregson's theory is specific to developed democracies and thus it is unclear how their theory might apply in a sub-par democracy, it is nevertheless instructive to explore whether the Internet influenced democratic satisfaction without changing how individuals actually rated the quality of their own democracy. If this were the case, it would suggest that, contrary to what mirror-holding and window-opening predict, the observed Internet effects are visceral in nature and therefore not primarily information-driven.

To address this, I test whether members of the Internet group tend to make more "accurate" evaluations of their democracy than members of the control group. Since what is truly an accurate evaluation is a subjective and complex determination, in this context "accurate" simply suggests that individuals changed their evaluation of the quality of the Bosnian democratic system in the same direction as their satisfaction (Hypothesis 2). To test this, I compared the answers that respondents in the Internet and control groups provided to the following survey question:

In your opinion, how much of a democracy is Bosnia today?
Possible Responses:
- Full democracy
- A democracy, but with minor problems
- A democracy, but with major problems
- Not a democracy

If the Internet's negative effect on democratic satisfaction is primarily information-driven, then the Internet group should believe that Bosnia is "less" of a democracy than the control group. In fact, as shown in table

A6.3, a two-sample *t*-test reveals that members of the Internet group did consider Bosnia to be less democratic than the control group (*p*-value ≤ .07). On average, the Internet group perceived Bosnia's level of democracy to be 6 percentage points lower than did the control group. This supports Hypothesis 2: Internet use encourages individuals to reevaluate the quality of democratic practices available in their country in the same direction as their change in satisfaction. Thus, the Internet's capacity to provide information that encourages individuals to reevaluate the quality of their own democracy does indeed appear to be driving its influence on democratic satisfaction, at least in part.

In an additional test related to Hypothesis 2, I asked respondents to rate their degree of trust in the Bosnian government. This enables a more specific test of the claim that the Internet provides users with information pertaining to their own government that causes them to reevaluate its democratic performance—in this case, the governments' accountability and commitment to those they were elected to serve. I also asked respondents to rate their degree of trust in the Bosnian press, which permits this analysis to consider whether Internet use simply encourages cynicism in general—suggesting that, rather than being information-driven, the Internet's negative effect on democratic satisfaction may in fact be better attributed to some sort of visceral reaction that promotes indiscriminate cynicism.

Accordingly, a two-sample *t*-test revealed that the amount of trust that members of the Internet group assigned to the Bosnian government was 10 percentage points less than that of the control group (*p*-value ≤ .05). Conversely, there was only marginal difference in the amount of trust that these two groups placed in the Bosnian press, which fell well outside the threshold for significance (difference = –.02, *p*-value ≤ .45). This supports the claim that the Internet provides users with information about their own government that individuals use to reevaluate their government's performance, shaping their satisfaction accordingly. Moreover, it does not appear that Internet exposure simply encourages across-the-board disillusionment or cynicism.

Does Internet Use Encourage Subscription to Norms Commonly Associated with High-Performing Democracies?

Scholars attributed the 1990s wave of democratization to "demonstration effects" in which enhanced international communication encouraged nations to follow the examples set by neighboring countries already on the path toward democratization (Huntington 1993). Additional scholars argue that international communication spreads liberal ideas and a humanistic culture, which favors a "democracy of rights" (Inglehart & Welzel 2005; Schudson 2004). While these are relevant and important considerations of additional potential effects of Internet use, the question of whether or not the Internet increases users' support for democracy as the preferred system of governance for their own countries is, for the moment, outside the scope of this discussion. Instead, window-opening merely contends that the Internet exposes individuals to a more globally consistent conception of what constitutes good democratic governance, dominated by the norms commonly associated with high-performing democracies.

This is important because there are several different ways to conceptualize democracy (G. Almond & Verba 1963; Dalton et al. 2007). Congruence theory, in turn, posits that democratic satisfaction is contingent on individuals' beliefs about what actually constitutes democracy (Anderson & Guillory 1997; Kornberg & Clarke 1994; Miller et al. 1997). The capacity to define democracy is a crucial component in shaping support for democratic governments, particularly those in transition. Therefore, exposure to information about how democracy functions in the advanced democracies that tend to dominate the Internet ought to restrict a government's latitude in defining the terms through which its own citizens conceptualize and evaluate the extent and quality of democratic practices available in their own nation. This will provide a more globally consistent metric for evaluations, shaping satisfaction with these democratic practices accordingly.

Finally, it is important to remember that, just because the international community does not consider a particular country to be democratic, this does not prohibit the leaders of these same countries from glorifying and propagandizing the existence of certain democratic practices, such as local elections or protection of human rights, to their own populations. The Internet's potential to reveal the large disjuncture between, on the one hand, how one's own government defines both itself and these democratic practices in general, and, on the other hand, how that government's (un) democratic character stands up against a more global measure of democratic performance, has important implications for the Internet's potential effect in democratizing and even nondemocratic countries. Recall that even China—widely considered among the least democratic of countries—insists on its own official website that it has made great strides in "respecting and safeguarding human rights with strengthening democracy."

This leads to Hypothesis 3, which predicts that Internet users in a developing democracy will be more likely to conceptualize democracy in terms of the democratic rights and norms generally associated with high-performing democracies. To test this, I compared the Internet and control groups' responses to a question asking how important they believe specific democratic principles commonly associated with high-performing democracies are to democracy in general. These norms include the right to vote, freedom of speech, freedom to be informed about the government, freedom to criticize the government, freedom to choose between candidates from different parties, and the right to gather and demonstrate. If the Internet exposes individuals to a more consistent global conception of democracy, then the Internet group should assign greater significance to these principles than the control group.

The results of the experiment indicate that across the board the Internet group rated the democratic principles generally associated with high-performing democracies to be more important than did members of the control group. In fact, the Internet group assigned more importance to *all six* core democratic principles (p-value $\leq$ .01 in every case). It thus appears that the Internet does indeed encourage users to conform to global norms regarding good democratic governance, as Hypothesis 3 predicts. This lends credence to the claim that the Internet provides users with a more globally consistent scale by which to make more reliable comparative evaluations regarding how well democracy functions in their own countries (see table A6.4).

What Does This Mean for Attitudes Regarding Democratization?

Thus far, the experiment findings support each of the hypotheses: the Internet decreased democratic satisfaction in Bosnia and Herzegovina's sub-par democracy, encouraged users to reevaluate the strength of the Bosnian democracy and the trustworthiness of their government, and encouraged individuals to assign greater importance to the democratic norms commonly associated with high-performing democracies. Internet optimists may conclude that these findings support the Internet's potential as a positive force for democratization. However, whether these effects actually translate into increased tolerance for the sometimes unpleasant and circuitous process of democratization is neither guaranteed nor automatic.

To test whether Internet exposure increased these individuals' commitment to the process of democratization, I compared the Internet and control groups' responses to the following question:

Which of the following statements is closest to your view?
Possible Responses
- Statement 1: Our present system of elected government should be given more time to deal with inherited problems.

- Statement 2: If our present system cannot produce results soon, we should try another form of government.
- Do not agree with either.
- Don't know

If the Internet increases commitment to democratization, then the Internet group should be more likely to agree with Statement 1. If the Internet neither increases nor decreases commitment, then members of the Internet group should not demonstrate a particular preference for either Statement 1 or 2 (i.e., should opt for either answer choice 3 or 4). But if the Internet decreases commitment to democratization, members of the Internet group should exhibit a stronger preference for Statement 2.

A two-sample t-test indicates that the Internet group was in fact 17 percentage points more likely to agree with Statement 2 (p-value $\leq .04$), thus revealing that exposure to the Internet decreased individuals' willingness to wait for the current "democratic" government to resolve the nation's problems. This lends credence to the European Stability Initiative's (2004) concern regarding the looming "temptation of authoritarianism" in Bosnia. It also suggests that exposure to the Internet may prove a double-edged sword in some cases: on the one hand enhancing the accuracy of citizens' assessments of their own democracies, while on the other hand increasing their willingness to consider alternative forms of governance if their own democracy is performing poorly (see table A6.5).

Conclusion

The results of this field experiment confirm the relationship uncovered by the previous chapters' analyses of cross-national survey data: the Internet depresses satisfaction with how democracy functions in a poorly performing democracy. This experiment also substantiates the Internet's effect on evaluations and democratic attitudes beyond satisfaction. In this case, Internet use lowered individuals' evaluations of the strength of democratic practices available in Bosnia as well as their assessments of the trustworthiness of their government officials. In addition, exposure to the Internet made individuals increasingly likely to conceptualize democracy in terms of the principles commonly associated with advanced democracies. Yet it also turns out that Internet use made individuals increasingly likely to consider abandoning the current elected system of government if the present problems cannot be resolved quickly. So what should Internet enthusiasts and skeptics make of this mixed bag of findings? First and foremost, that both camps may have it partially right.

Before leaving this discussion, however, it is important to consider a few caveats. First, as the social constructionist view (favored by this book) mandates, these specific findings should not be automatically assumed to apply to all other countries without testing. It may be the case, for example, that the increased willingness to forsake their current system of elected government is peculiar to Bosnia due to its particular political history as well as its recent war and very recent transition to democracy. Or it may simply be the case that this effect is contingent on the presence of the "looming threat of authoritarianism," which to varying degrees still pervades the national mindset of citizens living in many post-communist nations. If this is the case, it is less likely that citizens living in developing democracies without similar political and ideological histories will exhibit this reaction.

More generally, this mixed bag of findings clearly underscores the degree to which the theoretical framework undergirding the study of political Internet effects will benefit from conducting additional field experiments across a range of countries. As this body of research accumulates, scholars will be able to tease out and differentiate between the components of the Internet's political effects that are dependent on specific national contexts and those that are generalizable across borders. This will also provide insight into which social, cultural, historical, and political factors condition the effect of Internet use on political evaluations and satisfaction and which do not. This promises to provide the field with a much more nuanced and robust understanding of the precise mechanisms driving the effect of the Internet on political evaluations, behaviors, and even outcomes—a matter that remains in a black box at this time.

Appendix 6.1. The t-test Results for Chapter 6

TABLE A 6.1.   Paired *t*-test of the difference in satisfaction with democracy reported by the Internet group before and after Internet exposure

	Number of Observations	Mean Satisfaction	Standard Error	Standard Deviation	95% CI
Satisfaction with Democracy before Internet Exposure	55	32%	3	22	[26%, 38%]
Satisfaction with Democracy after Internet Exposure	55	29%	3	23	[23%, 35%]
Difference		–3	2		[–7, 1]

Probability (Pre-satisfaction > Post-satisfaction) = 92%
p-value ≤ .08*

TABLE A 6.2.   Two-sample *t*-test of the difference in satisfaction with democracy reported by the Internet and control groups

	Number of Observations	Mean Satisfaction	Standard Error	Standard Deviation	95% CI
Internet Group (excluding non-compliers)	55	28%	3	20	[22%, 34%]
Internet Group (including non-compliers)	57	30%	3	24	[24%, 35%]
Control Group	60	34%	3	22	[28%, 39%]

Probability (Internet Group satisfaction, excluding non-compliers < Control Group Satisfaction) = 91%*

Probability (Internet group satisfaction, including non-compliers < Control Group Satisfaction) = 84%

Note. For brevity's sake, the remaining *t*-test tables include all members of the Internet group (i.e., it does not exclude non-compliers who did not use the Internet during the two-month period). However, the results of the *t*-tests excluding non-compliers either maintain or increase in significance for each of the reported findings.

TABLE A 6.3.   How members of the Internet and control groups evaluate level of Bosnian democracy

	Number of Observations	Mean Level of Democracy	Standard Error	Standard Deviation	95% CI
Internet Group	57	37%	3	24	[37%, 49%]
Control Group	60	43%	3	17	[31%, 39%]
Difference		−6	2		
Probability (Internet Group Satisfaction < Control Group Satisfaction) = 93% *p*-value ≤ .07*					

TABLE A 6.4.   Importance of various rights to democracy in general

	Internet Group	Control	Difference
Right to Vote	.95 (*n* = 57, SE = .02)	.82 (*n* = 60, SE = .04)	.13 (*p*-value = .01)***
Freedom of Speech	.92 (*n* = 57, SE = .02)	.78 (*n* = 60, SE = .04)	.14 (*p*-value = .01)***
Freedom to Be Informed	87 (n = 57, SE = .02)	.72 (*n* = 60, SE = .03)	.15 (*p*-value = .01)***
Freedom to Criticize Government	.86 (*n* = 57, SE = .03)	.76 (*n* = 60, SE = .03)	.09 (*p*-value = .01)***
Freedom of Different Parties	.83 (*n* = 57, SE = .03)	.68 (*n* = 60, SE = .04)	.15 (*p*-value = .01) ***
Right to Gather and Demonstrate	.78 (*n* = 57, SE =.03)	.66 (*n* = 60, SE = .04)	.12 (*p*-value = .01)***

Note. SE = standard error.

TABLE A 6.5. Internet and control group agreement with statement that the current system should be abandoned if results not produced soon

	Number of Observations	Current System Should Be Abandoned	Standard Error	Standard Deviation	95% CI
Internet Group	53	57%	7	50	[43%, 70%]
Control Group	53	40%	7	49	[26%, 53%]
Difference		17%	10		[36, 2]

Probability (Internet Group Satisfaction > Control Group Satisfaction) = 96%
p-value ≤ .04**

CHAPTER 7

At the Internet Café
A Test for Effects in the Tanzanian Election

IN THIS CHAPTER, I present the results of a field experiment conducted in Tanzania in the months preceding their 2010 general election. Specifically, I test whether the Internet influenced individuals' perception of the fairness and integrity of the election and subsequent recount as well as related evaluations of the political system in Tanzania. Taking into account the number of protests, riots, and revolts sparked by contested or dubious electoral results, this is an important consideration of the Internet's capacity to alter the sort of evaluations that, in some instances, motivate individuals to act and organize politically.

The primary hypothesis motivating this experiment is that, as a result of mirror-holding, the Internet will depress evaluations of the fairness of the election and recount. Although Tanzania's traditional press is less restricted than that of most African countries, according to widely accepted measures of press freedom, there remains much room for improvement. Reporters Without Borders (2010) ranks Tanzania's degree of press freedom as 41st out of 178 countries as of 2010, while Freedom House (2010) still designates Tanzania as a Partly Free (as opposed to Free) country. Accordingly, the Internet should provide a different, more robust, and more critical set of information regarding the integrity of the Tanzanian election than the traditional media. Thus, I predict that Internet users will evaluate the integrity of the election and recount more critically.

In the following sections, I provide information about the context of the election, followed by a delineation of the procedure employed in this experiment. I then present the results of the test of the primary hypothesis regarding whether the Internet negatively influenced perceptions of a specific democratic process in Tanzania: the 2010 general election. I conclude with a consideration of several additional relevant findings—whether men and women differed in their Internet use and subsequent evaluations, whether Internet use influenced more general evaluations of Tanzania, and whether Internet users became more or less likely to vote in the election.

The 2010 General Election in Tanzania

After a five-day recount—which was demanded by the opposition when evidence of missing voters' names and insufficient voting materials at the polling stations surfaced—the incumbent candidate, President Jakaya Kikwete, won a second term with nearly 62 percent of the vote. The official report published by the Tanzania Election Monitoring Commission (TEMCO) painted the 2010 election as following a relatively peaceful campaign season, thanks in part to restraint showed by voters, political parties that worked to peacefully channel the enthusiasm of their supporters, and the presence of police officers who further helped keep the peace. However, the commission also acknowledged reports of physical combat between supporters of different parties, non-adherence to campaign timetables, and inequitable campaign spending and leveraging of other advantages (i.e., using state resources for campaign purposes) on behalf of the incumbent.

During the recount, the nation experienced minor rioting. Government officials identified lack of familiarity with recount guidelines and the new computerized counting system as the reasons for delay. Nevertheless, a number of voters feared that the delay was due to the recount having been rigged, which sparked violent skirmishes between police officers and protestors in some cases (TEMCO 2010). In all, although 2010 was a vast improvement over previous elections, it still fell well short of the threshold required to be considered a fully free and fair election.

It is also relevant to note the presence of Ushahidi, a non-profit tech company, on the ground and online in Tanzania in the days leading up to the election. Ushahidi, meaning "testimony" in Swahili, originated in Kenya as an online platform for mapping instances of violence after the contested election of 2008. Since this time, it has expanded its website to allow individuals across the globe to gather reports of various types of events through the Internet, text messages, and emails sent from the field, often from average citizens. These crowdsourced reports are then used to aggregate information and visually map online in (virtual) real-time the occurrence, frequency, and location of such events—from wildfires, to hate speech intended to incite violence, to electoral abuses (Internews Center for Innovation and Learning 2012).

In the case of the Tanzanian election, Ushahidi launched *Uchaguzi TZ,* which deployed 2,000 official monitors, used 30,000 trusted sources, and solicited reports from average citizens in order to aid in monitoring this election. A review of the posts made to Uchaguzi during the election mirror and multiply the offenses noted in the TEMCO report. Examples of these posts include "Campaign intimidation of female candidates," "Voters names missing from voter register," "Purchasing of voters cards," and "Media biased in reporting election campaings (*sic*)." The presence of Ushahidi during this election means that voters had access to concrete, real-time information via the Internet regarding electoral abuses in the days leading up to and following Election Day.

PROCEDURE

Participants were recruited in person at several congregation points throughout the community of Morogoro, a town of more than 200,000 residents located about 120 miles west of Dar es Salaam, the commercial capital of Tanzania. These congregation points include professional and trade schools, secondary schools, the main bus station, hair salons, and markets. Over a period of a week, my research assistant and I collected more than two hundred names and mobile phone numbers from individuals interested in participating. While there was a fairly high level of mobile phone penetration in the community, individuals without phones were still able to sign up with the phone number of a friend, family member, or neighbor. After the names were collected, we used a random number generator to assign 70 individuals to the experimental group (i.e., Internet group), 70 individuals to the control group, and the remainder to serve as alternates when members selected for the experimental or control groups could not be reached or no longer wished to participate.[1]

After random assignment, we called members of both groups and asked them to meet us at one of the two Internet cafés enlisted to serve as sites for this experiment, Valentine's Internet Café and Daus Internet Café. Once participants completed the consent form, we asked them to fill out pretest questionnaires, for which they were paid 3,000 TZS (equivalent to $2 USD). These pretests were brief and contained only a handful of questions pertaining to voting and evaluations of the Tanzanian government. In addition, the pretest contained a range of questions on other topics intended to mask the true focus of the study, such as questions about Tanzanian hip hop music and the national football team.

After completing the pretest questionnaires, the participants in the Internet group were set up with accounts at their assigned Internet café, where

I had pre-paid for each individual to receive 75 hours of Internet time to be used over the next two months. I also hired two additional assistants to offer participants in-depth tutorials on Internet use, including how to navigate from one page to another, conduct searches, and set up email accounts. Participants in the control group were not given Internet access at this time, but they were informed that they would be contacted again in two months, at which point they would receive an equitable amount of free Internet use.

As in the case of the Bosnian experiment, we made no effort to direct how the participants used the Internet over the next two months, nor did we electronically monitor their Internet use. We avoided such oversight in order to maximize external validity and to avoid infringing on privacy boundaries. Essentially, we wanted participants to use the Internet as they would naturally, without outside influence or guidance. When the two-month period concluded, my assistant and I contacted individuals in both the experimental and control groups by telephone and offered 3,000 TZS ($2 USD) to complete the post-treatment survey.

RESULTS

Commensurate with the expectations of random assignment, members of the Internet group and control groups did not differ significantly from one another in demographic terms. The average age of the participants in the experiment was 25 years old (standard deviation = 10 years); their education was completed, on average, at the age of 21, which is approximate to completing some secondary school or professional training (standard deviation = 3 years); 21 percent reported some form of current part-time or full-time employment; and 67 percent were male.

Clearly, the demographic profile of participants in this experiment tended to be younger, more often male, and more likely to be educated than the Tanzanian population at large. However, these demographics are highly reflective of the actual demographic profile of "early users" of the Internet in developing nations (Christensen & Levinson 2003). This further promotes the external validity of this study, since these participants share the same demographic profile as actual early Internet users in developing nations.

How Did They Use the Internet?

According to the records kept by the café owners, members of the Internet group spent an average of 42 hours on the Internet during the treatment period (with a standard deviation of 33 hours). According to self-reports gathered through the posttest questionnaires, 95 percent of the participants reported that they had an email address, 64 percent reported that they had a Facebook account, and 64 percent reported reading blogs while online. In addition, 61 percent of participants reported that they "mostly" used the Internet to look for information and news, 32 percent reported that they "mostly" used the Internet for social media (e.g., Facebook, Twitter, Myspace), and only 13 percent stated that they "mostly" used the Internet for entertainment (e.g., to watch videos on YouTube, to listen to music). Finally, 15 percent of participants stated that they regularly followed election information on the Internet, and 22 percent said they followed election information online some of the time.

Regarding whether participants primarily visited Tanzania-specific, Africa-specific, or Western-specific websites, the majority of participants expressed a preference for websites from a wide range of sources. Only 17 percent of the participants reported that they mostly frequented Tanzania websites, and 23 percent indicated that they mostly visited non-Tanzanian sites, with the remaining 60 percent reporting that they preferred to visit both Tanzanian and non-Tanzanian websites. Moreover, only 14 percent of individuals reported that they preferred to exclusively frequent Western-based websites, with 18 percent reporting a strong preference for African-based websites, and the remaining 65 percent indicated that their Internet diet regularly consisted of both Western and African websites.

In summary, the fact that over one-third of the participants specifically sought out information about the election online, and nearly two-thirds reported mostly using the Internet to gather news and information, diminishes doubts regarding individuals' desire to seek out information about their own governments while online. Thus, the findings generated by this field experiment provide valuable insight into how actual individuals in developing nations use the Internet. It is clear that even when left to their own devices, a substantial portion of individuals in developing countries do, in fact, use the Internet as a tool for seeking out political information.

Did the Internet Influence Evaluations of the Election?

Regarding the primary hypothesis in this chapter—whether the Internet negatively influenced participants' evaluations of a contested election—using a two-sample t-test, members of the Internet group were 15 percentage points less likely to believe that the election was conducted fairly and impartially (p-value $\leq .04$). This does not necessarily mean that they were more likely to state definitively that the election was conducted unfairly, however. Rather, individuals in the Internet group who were not willing to state that the election was fair were about equally as likely to answer "Don't Know" (33%) as to state that the election was actually unfair (25%). Nevertheless, it is clear that members of the Internet group were less certain of the fairness and the impartiality of the election compared to their peers in the control group. (See table A7.1. Note that all *t*-test tables for this chapter are included in appendix 7.1.) As for perceptions of the recount, members of the Internet group were more likely to definitively believe that the recount was conducted unfairly compared to the control group by 12 percentage points (p-value $\leq$ .06). (See table A7.2.)

In sum, these results support the primary hypothesis motivating this chapter. Internet users were less certain of the fairness of the election as well as more critical of the fairness of the subsequent recount, compared to individuals in the control group. Considering the violent protests sparked by a contested election in neighboring Kenya in 2007, the Internet's capacity to make individuals more critical of the integrity of electoral results can have real and profound consequences. However, as will be revealed in the discussion of the Internet's effect on voting behavior, one democratic gain (such as greater transparency of a sub-par democratic process) does not necessarily or always produce other prodemocratic changes in behavior.

Did Internet Use and Its Effect Differ between Men and Women?

A future avenue this line of research should pursue includes identifying and testing demographic characteristics that likely mediate or condition the Internet's effect on evaluations. For example, in the case of this experiment, male participants in the Internet group were substantially more likely to believe that the election and recount were unfair than were their female counterparts, by differentials of 25 percent and 27 percentage points (p-values $\leq$ .05 and .01, respectively). In the control group, men were also more likely to doubt the integrity of the election and recount as compared to women in the control group; however, this differential spanned a much smaller margin and did not always reach statistical significance, at 12 percent and 15 percentage points (p-values $\leq$ .13 and .1, respectively).

Interestingly, compared to their female counterparts, men in the Internet group were also more likely to report following news about the election online (by 20 percentage points) and using the Internet primarily to gather news and information (by 26 percentage points). Thus, future research will help better delineate whether specific demographic characteristics, such as gender, make individuals particularly prone to Internet effects and whether this relationship is direct, mediated by how those demographic characteristics determine Internet use, or some combination of both.

Did the Internet Influence General Democratic Satisfaction?

At first glance, Internet exposure does not appear to have exerted a significant effect on general democratic satisfaction—although, in substantive terms, Internet users did differ in satisfaction in the direction predicted by this analysis. Specifically, the percentage of satisfied members of the Internet group is 6 percentage points lower than that of the control group; however, this difference does not quite reach statistical significance (p-value ≤ .2). Changes in general democratic satisfaction between the pretest and posttest also move in directions that accord with the theory guiding this analysis. Whereas mean general satisfaction among members of the Internet group decreased by 2 percentage points over this period, mean satisfaction actually increased among members of the control group over this same period by 5 percentage points. However, this 7-point differential also falls just outside significance (p-value ≤ .19).

This raises the important question of the degree to which temporal and contextual factors may further condition the effect of the Internet on democratic attitudes. To what degree, for example, does the excitement surrounding an election and the psychic gratification of casting a vote condition the Internet's effect on general satisfaction in this context? These findings suggest that the experience of an election may increase general satisfaction among non-Internet users but that this context-specific effect may be dampened or even reversed by Internet use during this same period. Internet use may moderate election-specific influences on democratic attitudes. If so, how long is such an effect is likely to last?

Examining and testing the effect of Internet use at a more nuanced level could shed useful light on a broader range of factors that likely condition the Internet's effect on satisfaction and related political evaluations, particularly in a high-salience context such as an election. In this case, a more nuanced consideration reveals that members of the Internet group were more polarized in terms of their general democratic (dis)satisfaction than members of the control group. More specifically, a variance ratio test reveals that members of the Internet group were more polarized in their democratic satisfaction *after* the election than were members of the control group (difference in standard deviations = 6, p-value ≤ .12). (See table A7.3). While this differential falls just outside of significance, it is nevertheless worthwhile to note, since it suggests that this polarization may be a result of Internet use during the election—a variance ratio test of general democratic satisfaction *before* the election shows no significant difference between the Internet and control groups (difference in standard deviations = 2, p-value ≤ .37).

In sum, it is likely that there are a multitude of factors—from temporal, context-specific factors to more enduring fixtures of a nation's social and political systems—that condition the effect of Internet use on satisfaction and related political evaluations. In this case, Internet use may have contributed to the polarization of individuals' general democratic satisfaction over the course of the election. This lends tentative support to the literature discussed in chapter 3, which posits that Internet use may be increasing polarization (Stroud 2008; Sunstein 2001), at least in certain contexts or among certain segments of the population of Internet users. This set of findings also demonstrates why it is useful to look for Internet effects at a more nuanced level as well as at how specific contexts—such as a high-salience event like an election—may further condition the effect of Internet use on various democratic attitudes.

Did Internet Use Effect Trust?

A set of related political evaluations may now be considered: How did the Internet affect individuals' trust in specific governmental and social institutions? Did Internet use, for example, highlight the deficit of available information through traditional news outlets, diminishing their trust in Tanzanian news outlets? In support of this supposition, the study found that members of the Internet group were 9 percentage points less likely to indicate that they trusted the Tanzanian news media (p-value $\leq .07$). Thus, it is possible that exposure to the broader and more diverse array of perspectives about the election online may have highlighted the relative dearth and slant of information provided by the traditional media.

It is worthwhile to recall, however, that this diminished trust in the press as a result of Internet use was not evident in the experiment in Bosnia and Herzegovina. This once again raises the useful question of whether there are particular features of the relationships between these two national presses and their respective governments and citizens that might condition the effect of the Internet on trust of the national media. Or is there something specific about being in an election that may exert a temporal, context-specific effect on Internet users' evaluations of the integrity of their national press?

It does not appear that distrust of the traditional news media necessarily extended to government institutions in Tanzania. Instead, also unlike the Bosnian experiment, the difference between the Internet group and the control group in how much trust members placed in the political parties and the government as a whole fell well outside the range of statistical significance. This once again underscores the need to conduct more research to uncover the national and contextual factors that condition the effect of Internet use on related political evaluation.

The exception to the lack of an effect of Internet use on trust toward the government, however, is the finding that members of the Internet group were *more* likely to trust the Tanzanian police force by 12 percentage points (p-value $\leq$ .1). Recall that the police force played a central and visible role during both the election and the recount in terms of making sure that the election was conducted fairly—such as arresting individuals caught with multiple vote cards—but also in containing the protests and violent outbreaks in the days before and after the election. This has interesting implications, therefore, for how the Internet may have captured and highlighted the police force's activities during the election.

Did the Internet Influence People's Decision to Vote?

At the outset of the experiment in August, members of the Internet and control groups reported approximately the same level of intention to vote in the upcoming election. Specifically, among those who reported that they were eligible to vote, 65 percent of the members of the Internet group reported on the pre-survey that they definitely planned to vote, while 68 percent of the control group reported the same. However, after the two-month period on the Internet, significantly fewer members of the Internet group reported actually voting compared to the control group. In fact, members of the Internet group were 11 percentage points less likely to vote (p-value $\leq$ .09). (See table A7.4.)

Thus, although both groups reported similar intentions to vote during the initial stages of the experiment, after the two-month period online, members of the Internet group became significantly less likely to vote compared to members of the control group who were not online. Taking into account that members of the Internet group were also significantly less likely to believe the election was conducted fairly and impartially, this suggests that although the Internet may have equipped these individuals with more robust information on which to base their evaluations of the integrity of the election, this democratic boon may carry a negative side effect. In this case, Internet users who became more aware of electoral abuses also became less likely to vote—a troubling finding for those who subscribe to the importance of participatory democracy.

One interpretation is that members of the Internet group became more cynical about whether their vote mattered. After all, the belief that an election is not being conducted fairly can produce two very divergent responses—while some people may respond by protesting and taking to the streets, others may simply throw up their hands and stay home. In this case, individuals did in fact become less likely to turn out, suggesting that they responded in the latter manner. However, interestingly, members of the Internet group were not turned off from the political process entirely: both groups were about equally likely to participate in a campaign event—82 percent of members of the control group reported attending at least one campaign event or meeting, while 78 percent of members of the Internet group reported doing the same.

This raises two important considerations. First, what factors predict when and where more critical evaluations of sub-par democratic processes will translate into prodemocratic behavior and organization offline, and which predict when it will simply lead to greater apathy and enervation? The second consideration is whether, then, both Internet skeptics and optimists have it partially right, and the Internet will prove a double-edged sword for democracy and democratization. Both of these considerations are examined in more detail in the following chapter.

Appendix 7.1. The t-test Results for Chapter 7

TABLE A 7.1.   Two-sample *t*-test of the difference in the percentage of individual that believed the election was conducted fairly and impartially

	Number of Observations	% Who Believed Election Fair	Standard Error	Standard Deviation	95% CI
Internet Group	60	42%	6	50	[29%, 55%]
Control Group	65	57%	6	50	[45%, 69%]
Difference		−15			[−2, 33]
	Probability (Internet Group < Control Group) = 96% *p*-value = .04**				

TABLE A 7.2. Two-sample *t*-test of the difference in the percentage of individual that believed the recount was *not* conducted fairly and impartially

	Number of Observations	% Believing Recount Not Fair	Standard Error	Standard Deviation	95% CI
Internet Group	59	27%	6	45	[15%, 39%]
Control Group	65	15%	5	36	[6%, 24%]
Difference		12			[−26, 3]

Probability (Internet Group > Control Group) = 94%
p-value = .06*

TABLE A 7.3. Variance ratio test of general democratic satisfaction between members of the Internet group and control group

	Number of Observations	% Satisfied with Democracy	Standard Error	Standard Deviation	95% CI
Internet Group	62	82%	5	39	[72%, 92%]
Control Group	65	88%	4	33	[80%, 96%]

Probability (Variance for Internet Group > Variance for Control Group) = 88%
p-value = .12

TABLE A 7.4. Two-sample *t*-test of the difference in voter turnout for those in the Internet and control groups

	Number of Observations	Mean Democratic Satisfaction	Standard Error	Standard Deviation	95% CI
Internet Group	59	66%	6	48	[54%, 79%]
Control Group	58	78%	5	42	[67%, 89%]
Difference		−12%	8		[−5, 28]

Probability (Internet Group < Control Group) = 91%
p-value = .09*

CHAPTER 8

Both Sides Now
Democratic Reflections and Illusions

THIS BOOK has explored an important yet largely understudied component of the Internet's potential to motivate political activity by testing
whether Internet use affects citizens' satisfaction regarding the quality of
democratic practices in their country. The Internet's capacity to uniquely affect citizens' political evaluations is a result of the profound degree to which
it has reshaped contemporary information landscapes. Thanks to its mirror-
holding and window-opening functions, the Internet alters the quantity and
range of information as well as the criteria through which individuals assess
their governments. This is significant because it is these evaluations that can
and will at times encourage citizens to act and organize politically.

After all, the decision to act and organize begins in the minds of men and
women. As Davies explains, "The discriminatory and integrative responses,
including the decision-making process as it relates to all action, including
the political, takes place in the brain, causing the body to act" (1997, 6).
Thus, while the majority of extant research explores the Internet's political
effects on more tangible democratic behaviors and outcomes—which have
tended to yield mixed results—the present analysis makes a valuable contribution to the existing body of research by demonstrating the import of
better understanding the Internet's effect on the less tangible, more antecedent and psychological components of its political effects.

In brief review, the first chapter set the stage for this analysis by considering the political implications of how the digital information revolution
is changing the information and criteria that individuals use to evaluate
their governments—across democratic, democratizing, and non-democratic
countries. This is an important component of understanding the Internet's
potential political effects since not only does this new information land-

scape alter the task of day-to-day governance, but it also influences the types of evaluations that can encourage individuals to act and organize to effect political change.

The second chapter outlined in detail the mirror-holding and window-opening functions, the primary mechanisms driving Internet's influence on users' evaluations of and satisfaction with the quality of democracy provided by their government. Thanks to mirror-holding, the Internet provides citizens with more information than traditional media—in terms of quantity and range—with which to evaluate their governments. One important component of this is the way the Internet visibly documents and aggregates instances of government failure and malfeasance at the national level, encouraging citizens to link individual grievances to a broader national trend. Window-opening, in turn, exposes Internet users to more information about how democracy functions in other nations, altering the expectations and criteria that guide citizens' evaluative processes. An important consequence of this is that Internet use encourages individuals to adhere to more globally consistent metrics with which to evaluate their own government's performance.

Chapter 3 considered potential limitations of mirror-holding and window-opening. This included a discussion of the degree to which less formalized cyber warfare tactics employed by governments discourage activism and critical discussion online; the degree to which state-sponsored propaganda and misinformation Internet campaigns can effectively drown out or distort independent content online; the potential restrictions imposed by the digital divide; whether mobile phones are really the technology that is having the most meaningful impact in developing countries; and whether there is actually too much choice between content online. In the end, although it is certain that each of these do somewhat distort mirror-holding and window-opening to varying degrees across different countries, it is also clear that their capacity to obscure or becloud the mirror and window provided by the Internet is limited.

In chapters 4 and 5, a multiple-level approach that encompassed different data sets at different levels of analysis confirmed the Internet's capacity to influence various evaluations meaningful to the cost-benefit calculus that guides political activity. Specifically, the tests supported the primary hypothesis guiding this analysis: the direction of the Internet's effect on democratic satisfaction is conditioned by the actual quality of democratic practices available in that country. This means that Internet use caused individuals to become increasingly dissatisfied in nations with weak democratic practices but more satisfied in nations with robust democratic practices. Additionally, chapters 6 and 7 also demonstrated the effect of the Internet on related political evaluations, including the quality of democracy available in one's nation, trust in one's government and other national institutions, the terms through which individuals conceptualize democracy, whether individuals perceived democracy as the preferred system of governance for their country, and whether the Internet influenced individuals' perception of the fairness of a controversial election.

Overall, the findings in this book confirm the Internet's capacity to influence meaningful political evaluations. The take-away with perhaps the greatest potential consequence for political activity is that the Internet encourages citizens to become more critical of a poorly performing government across a range of related evaluations. In addition to the potential for these evaluations to motivate political activity and organization in the short term, it also suggests another more long-term, potentially prodemocratic outcome: the capacity to increase governmental transparency and accountability. In the new information landscape it will be more difficult for governments to hide transgressions or incompetence, suggesting a trend toward greater governmental responsiveness, if only out of the desire to avoid the potential repercussions of an agitated citizenry.

However, much work remains in identifying and testing the factors that determine when and where these more critical evaluations will actually produce tangible political activity, organization, and outcomes. As part of this effort, it is important that researchers acknowledge that the seeming boon of more informed and critical evaluations of poorly performing governments does not mean that all other political evaluations that follow will automatically and invariably be prodemocratic. Rather, in some instances the full range of the Internet's effects on evaluations, and thus on activity, will likely prove to be a double-edged sword for democratization and democracy. For example, the experiment in Bosnia and Herzegovina revealed that individuals who became more skeptical of and dissatisfied with the quality of democratic practices in their country also became more likely to consider alternative forms of government as preferable for their country. And in Tanzania, voters who became more critical of the integrity of their contested presidential election were also less likely to vote.

The double-edged nature of the Internet's effects revealed in this analysis support the widening view that the results of information technology are not predetermined, but rather they depend on the decisions and intentions of those who utilize that technology, which are often themselves the product of a complex set of historical, societal, cultural, and personal factors. Castells (1996) points out that "the social dimension of the Information Technology Revolution seems bound to follow the law on the relationship between technology and society proposed some time ago by Melvin Krazenberg: 'Krazenberg's First Law reads as follows: Technology is neither good, nor bad, nor neutral.' . . the complex matrix of interaction between the technological forces unleashed by our species . . . are matters of inquiry rather than of fate" (65, emphasis original).

In light of this, constructing a more robust theoretical foundation of the Internet's effect on political evaluations, and thus on political activity and organization, is a necessary but complex endeavor. One potent avenue for future research in this vein entails expanding and refining how researchers operationalize Internet penetration. In a recent contribution to the field, Nisbet and Stoycheff (2014) break apart the measurement of Internet penetration into three distinct measures: the availability of hardware, the number of users, and the capacity of the bandwidth. It is likely that each of these features of Internet penetration will condition, to some degree, the quantity and quality of information available to citizens in a given nation, which will also have implications for the relative strength of the Internet's mirror-holding and window-opening functions in determining the set of information and criteria that individuals use to evaluate their governments. Thus, future research would benefit from expanding this effort to theorize and study the effects of these different components of Internet penetration.

More generally, the impetus belongs to researchers to continue to seek out and test the contextual factors that condition the Internet's effect across a broad range of politically relevant evaluations. It is also useful to investigate the factors that predict when the Internet's influence on a set of political evaluations will tend to be largely prodemocratic in nature, and when it will prove more of a mixed bag. Finally, each of these lines of inquiry is an important component of generating more reliable predictions of when and where these evaluations will make political activity and organization more or less likely to occur. Thus, the remainder of this chapter offers specific suggestions for the direction of future research in this vein.

A Closer Look at Mirror-Holding and Window-Opening

As the findings from this research demonstrate, there is clear value in studying the Internet's effects on attitudes and evaluations. By better understanding the nature of individuals' psychological reactions to different types of Internet use, researchers will better be able to predict how those reactions will shape political evaluations and satisfaction. As part of this effort, it would be beneficial to investigate the mirror-holding and window-opening functions in much more detail.

For example, what exactly do these uses of the Internet look like for different individuals across different countries? Is there a different effect of deliberate versus inadvertent exposure to the Internet's mirror-holding versus window-opening functions? Perhaps most importantly, what is the respective influence of each of these mechanisms on the evaluative process? Are there types of evaluations that are more likely to rely on mirror-holding versus window-opening, and vice versa? If so, do these distinct sets of evaluations have different staying power or possess different gravity as potential catalysts for political activity? Basically, researchers need to get inside users' heads to better understand these different types of Internet use and, more importantly, how each affects specific components of the evaluative process.

I tend to see mirror-holding and window-opening as two overlapping, shifting spectrums—much like a slide rule—with individuals' evaluative processes positioned somewhere along these distributions. The relative degree to which each function factors into a particular individual's evaluative process will likely vary across individuals, countries, points in time, and types of evaluations. While in some cases Internet users may be primarily influenced by the Internet's capacity to provide more information about their own government, in others users may be predominantly influenced by its capacity to expose them to information about how governments function in other countries.

Some of the personal characteristics that plausibly influence the degree to which an individual employs one function over another likely include political interest and engagement, age, education, literacy, technological aptitude, English proficiency, and sense of being a global citizen. The country-level factors, in turn, might consist of the geographic size and position of that country, various cultural and geopolitical factors, the number of country-specific and language-specific websites, and a government's censorship policies. As for the factors that will make these functions more or less pertinent to specific types of evaluations, most obviously these will pertain to whether the issues and information relevant to that evaluative process are largely domestic, transnational, or global in nature.

Identifying the Factors That Condition the Internet's Influence on Evaluations

In general, future research should seek to identify and test additional factors that condition the Internet's influence on evaluative processes. This will allow researchers to delineate the cases in which the Internet is likely to produce uniform effects across countries and those in which the direction of the Internet's effect will be determined by specific national contexts. This endeavor will also reveal the factors that predict when the full set of the Internet's effect on evaluation will trend in the prodemocratic direction and those that will encourage evaluations that are either antidemocratic in nature or, at least, a hindrance to democracy and democratization. The final and perhaps most important stage in this line of research entails identifying and testing the factors that will determine when these evaluations will be more or less likely to produce tangible political activity. Factors related to features of the national culture, the political system, and the state of the economy in these countries would likely be a fruitful place to start such an investigation.

Beginning with cultural factors, there are several dimensions of the national culture that may condition the Internet's effect on specific meaningful political evaluations. For example, to what degree have individuals come to accept some level of "corruption" as a necessary cost of doing business in their country? Whatever information the Internet provides about the extent of corruption perpetrated by members of the government will likely be filtered through citizens' notions of what constitutes "corruption"—a concept that is both ambiguous and nationally variable.

Another potentially meaningful cultural factor may be the degree to which individuals in that country share a sense of personal agency. For example, consider the Arabic expression *Inshallah* (if Allah wills it) commonly used in many Middle Eastern countries in response to questions regarding future endeavors. Some scholars (e.g., Patai 2002) claim that this expression is indicative of a shared sense of fatalism in these nations, suggesting relatively lower levels of a sense of personal agency and efficacy among the citizenry. While this conclusion is controversial and certainly a blatant overgeneralization, it does raise the question of whether the degree to which a nation's culture tends to view events or the actions of individuals as inevitable or as God's will may condition the circumstances that predict when evaluations will precipitate action.

For example, consider the question asked by the Pew Global Attitudes Project's 2011 survey of twenty-three different countries in which respondents were asked to indicate their agreement or disagreement with the following statement: "Success in life is determined by forces outside of our control." Whereas nearly four-fifths of respondents in India, Turkey, and Germany agreed with this statement, fewer than half of the British and Brazilian respondents surveyed agreed with this same statement. True to their reputation as individualists, Americans indicated the lowest level of agreement with this statement—with nearly two-thirds of Americans in disagreement.

Of course, this also raises a consideration of which attitudes this question is really measuring. To what degree, for example, is this survey question also reflecting attitudes about individual responsibility versus the appropriate role of the state, particularly in regard to social and economic policy? In any case, this alternative conceptualization also has potentially interesting implications regarding when and where heightened dissatisfaction as a result of Internet use is likely to motivate political organization and activity.

As for features related to a nation's political system, consider the role that political history and institutional memory may play in conditioning the effect of the Internet. For example, perhaps the Bosnian skepticism toward democracy as the appropriate system of governance for their nation is a reaction that is common to citizens of post-communist countries. In these countries scholars have noted a "looming temptation of authoritarianism" and a skepticism regarding the capacity of the mass public to participate effectively in policy formation. Thus, it is possible that citizens in democratizing countries without this communist heritage may be less likely to consider alternative forms of governance as viable. Other potential political factors that may condition the effect of the Internet on the direction and content of evaluations may include whether the country has a colonial heritage (and, if so, the nation of the colonizer), the structure of the national party system, inherited notions about patronage and the welfare state, recent experience with civil violence or war, the sense of a pressing and proximate external threat to the nation, and the degree to which that country has come to count on international aid.

Finally, consider the various economic factors that likely condition the effect of the Internet on a range of evaluations. First, the state of the economy itself is a rather strong indicator of the competence of the national government, and information and discussion about it will likely be reflected online. Moreover, when an economy is faring poorly, how responsibility for that failure is attributed in the national discussion will also likely condition evaluations. The capacity for the economy to shape general assessments of governments and their officials is substantiated by the large body of research identifying the factors that determine how (and whether) citizens cast their votes. Economic considerations consistently rank as one of the most powerful predictors of vote choice (Fiorina 1978; Kinder & Kiewiet 1981).

In support of this, an additional regression of the country-level data utilized in chapter 4, in which I employ an interaction of the Human Development Index (HDI) score and Internet penetration, reveals that quality of life does exert a contingent effect on democratic satisfaction similar to the contingent effect of the quality of a nation's democratic practices tested in this book. However, the substantive size and significance of the conditioning effect of quality of life on democratic satisfaction is somewhat smaller than that of quality of democratic practices (.2 and p-value ≤ .04 compared to .27 and p-value ≤ .01, based on a linear combination of the interaction coefficients). This is not surprising, since democratic satisfaction is logically more likely to be directly conditioned by the quality of democratic practices available in one's nation, which is more germane and directly related to assessments of democratic satisfaction. However, for the reasons discussed above, it is also not surprising that quality of life figures into this evaluative process to some degree. This also suggests that quality of life considerations are likely to condition some political evaluations more directly and substantially than others.

On a related aside, considering the near collapse of the global financial system that began in 2008 and continued to enfeeble global markets as of 2013, when I wrote this chapter, I suspected that the positive effect of the Internet on democratic satisfaction in advanced democracies would have diminished after 2008, as economic woes continued to grow in these countries. Essentially, I assumed that things may have gotten so bad in recent years economically that even in advanced democracies the Internet would now depress satisfaction with governments' performances. After all, much of the discussion online regarding the financial collapse points to an unregulated and self-serving banking industry, to whose transgressions government officials were only too happy to turn a blind eye, as a primary catalyst for the collapse.

To test for this, I searched for post-2008 public opinion data in these countries. As of the writing of this book, the only such data publicly available were from 2010 in the Latinobarometer and Eurobarometer surveys. I fully expected this data to reveal across-the-board dissatisfaction, even in advanced democracies. However, exactly the same relationship from the original time-series analysis continued in a cross-sectional analysis of 2010 data (reaching significance at the .01 level). In top-ranked democracies, expanded Internet penetration still predicted enhanced satisfaction; whereas, below this threshold, increased Internet expansion was still correlated with greater dissatisfaction.

Although I was pleased to see the original relationship reaffirmed by the 2010 data, I was surprised by this finding. Had things simply not gotten bad enough yet in 2010? Or, at least, had public discussion not turned harshly enough toward these governments for failing to stave off the crisis and then fumbling in their attempt to mitigate the fallout? Thanks to the Occupy movement that began in the United States and then expanded to other countries, by 2011 public discourse had become manifestly critical toward the special privileges the banking industry and other corporations enjoy, often to the detriment of the general population. Public opinion had also grown increasingly critical of the government's various failures in regulation and balancing budgets. So perhaps 2012 data would show something different? Or, is it the case that individuals are still making comparative evaluations with other countries, as window-opening predicts? Although things may be bad in advanced democracies relative to the years just before the collapse, conditions in these countries are still not nearly as bad as the conditions that citizens face in the majority of other countries so that perhaps individuals in advanced democracies nevertheless remain relatively satisfied.

In addition to addressing these questions, it seems likely that there are a number of additional economic indicators worth exploring. These include unemployment, change in real disposable income, economic inequality, the tax structure, and growth of GDP. Moreover, this research should also explore whether individuals are influenced by the simple level of these indicators, by comparative evaluations to other countries, or by retrospective evaluations in which the nation's trajectory matters most (and, if retrospective, how long is the time horizon of these comparisons). Finally, as mentioned above, there are likely a range of related political evaluations that are likely conditioned more directly by these economic indicators than democratic satisfaction, which should be explored more fully.

When Will Evaluations Translate to Political Activity?

The question of when and where evaluations will prompt political activity and organization is perhaps the most important component of the Internet's political effects. However, it cannot be answered fully until we better understand the influence of the Internet on those political evaluations. Nevertheless, before concluding it is worthwhile to briefly venture into this territory by first grounding this discussion in the classic argument offered by Davies (1971) regarding when men and women are more likely to revolt. According to Davies, two specific types of evaluations make revolt more likely. The first is a sense of a deprivation of basic needs, and the second is a belief that a government's laws and/or officials have violated equal justice. After all, if these types of evaluations are powerful enough to drive individuals to undertake the costly and extreme act of revolting in some instances, they are also likely to motivate a range of less-costly forms of political activity and organization in other instances.

As discussed previously, thanks to mirror-holding and window-opening, it is likely that the Internet will influence both of these evaluative processes. For example, the Internet's capacity to provide users with more globally consistent metrics with which to evaluate their own governments may prove instrumental in changing individuals' sense of what constitutes "basic needs." Recall that Internet users in Bosnia and Herzegovina became more likely to conceptualize democracy in terms of the norms and rights commonly associated with advanced democracies. Also recall the results produced by the country-level analysis, which suggest that it is the protection of civil liberties, rather than the presence of certain political processes or institutions, that more strongly conditions the Internet's effect on satisfaction.

So the question is, if the Internet makes individuals more likely to conceptualize democracy in terms of the protection of these civil liberties, at what point will individuals embrace these as "basic needs"? And, in those cases, when will individuals perceive the absence of these rights as a deprivation—thus sparking political activity? It is unlikely that this will be an automatic or inevitable outcome in every case; however, it will likely occur in some cases. Thus, identifying the factors that will predict when individuals will be more likely to perceive these civil liberties as basic needs would make a valuable contribution to the literature. There are other avenues beyond civil liberties through which the Internet likely influences citizens' sense of what constitutes basic needs and for determining when these needs are lacking that are worth consideration. Some of these may include quality and provision of public goods, such as electricity and running water, or opportunities for advancement, such as education and employment.

Turning to the second evaluation—a sense of unequal justice perpetrated by one's government—consider the Internet's mirror-holding function, through which the Internet provides a visible platform with which citizens can aggregate and document instances of government abuse, failure, and malfeasance. One significant result of this is that it will encourage individuals not to "morselize" their own experiences of government failure, encouraging them instead to link these experiences to a larger, entrenched national problem. Thus, when the mirror reflects a picture of widespread government malfeasance and abuse, this will likely give citizens a shared sense that their nation's laws and officials are unjust—making individuals more likely to perceive political activity as necessary to redress that injustice. For example, recall that the most common catalyst for uprisings since the latter decades of the twentieth century has been the unjust killing of a civilian by a government. Also recall how the Internet's capacity to widely and instantly relay evocative and grisly accounts of these killings—often through pictures of the corpses or of bereaved loved ones—suggests the unique capacity for the Internet to disseminate powerful, graphic information regarding the true human costs of injustice.

Finally, political scientist W. Lance Bennett (2007) offers a new view of citizenship in the digital age that has clear implications for when and where evaluations derived from Internet use may be more or less likely to precipitate political activity. Bennett sees the new generation, who came of age in the Internet world, increasingly demonstrating a preference to participate in the political realm as *actualizing citizens,* as opposed to the more traditional *dutiful citizens.* Whereas the dutiful citizen felt an obligation to participate politically, tended to view voting as the penultimate political act, learned about politics primarily from the traditional mass media, and belonged to traditional civic associations and parties; the actualizing citizen instead favors an individual sense of purpose over a sense of obligation to the government, sees alternative forms of participation (e.g., volunteering, activism, consumerism) as just as (if not more) meaningful as voting, distrusts the traditional media, and favors loose networks of peers connected by social media rather than membership in traditional organizations.

If this is the direction that citizenship is moving, what does this suggest about the potential for Internet use to shape evaluations that then motivate these citizens to act politically? First, it is clear that the Internet provides a venue for the discussion and sharing of relevant political information that will shape meaningful evaluations by connecting individuals to that network of trusted peers. Thus, when the discussion coursing through these networks begins to link specific political activities as remedies or appropriate responses to failures in governments' performances, this has the potential to catalyze those evaluations into action. Moreover, since the range of politically meaningful activities is broader than just voting, these networks can embrace and advocate for a variety of activities, many of which can also be carried out online—such as signing a petition, emailing a representative, boycotting a product, or donating to a cause.

There is the question, however, of how effective these alternative forms of political activity really are. Essentially, actualizing citizens may find it easier to engage in a range of political activities online, but how many of these activities really make a tangible difference in political outcomes? For example, it is evident that U.S. congressmen receive a torrent of emails on a daily basis from their constituents. What is not clear is how much weight these congressmen actually assign to these emails in the course of policy making.

If these are actualizing citizens, who are primarily motivated by a sense of individual purpose, there is also a question of what level of stimulus it will take to motivate them to action. Essentially, how dissatisfied and critical must these citizens become before they will find it worthwhile to act? Relatively speaking, it is not yet clear whether it is more or less difficult to motivate political activity from citizens who are motivated by a sense of individual purpose rather than a sense of obligation. For example, does this new form of individualized citizenship undercut the normative mechanisms of oversight that enable community members to punish or shame peers who decline to act? On the other hand, does social media and Internet use increase the capacity to reward political activity by giving individuals a venue to post and receive accolades for acting?

Finally, there is the question of when these more critical evaluations will be more likely to convince citizens to simply give up and check out politically, driven by a shared sense of futility or cynicism. After all, as Bennett reports, actualizing citizens put less faith in traditional media as well as in traditional political organizations and institutions. So does this mean that more critical evaluations derived from Internet use, in some instances, will encourage these actualizing citizens to increasingly turn away from engagement in the political process?

Speaking to how these critical evaluations might change the process of political organization in the Internet age, Shirky (2008) cogently describes how political organization has become increasingly efficient, thanks to tools provided by social media and new technology. For instance, the organizational costs associated with collective action are significantly reduced in the Internet age. This enables individuals to organize around issues and goals with minimal transaction costs and thus renders formal managerial oversight and traditional institutions less necessary to coordinate and sustain such organization.

So how do evaluations fit into this picture? Most obviously, if the Internet prompts greater dissatisfaction and more critical evaluations, would-be organizers will have a larger body of disaffected individuals to appeal to more efficiently and cheaply, who will likely be more receptive to arguments about the need for change and thus the need to organize. However, the success of such solicitations will likely depend on how effectively would-be organizers can focus and sustain that discontent around a specific problem and an appropriate remedy for that problem.

This necessarily suggests that there must be an individual (or group of individuals) willing to invest in organizing these disaffected citizens. Basically, if someone is not willing to marshal, coordinate, and direct this dissatisfaction toward a common purpose, it seems unlikely that these more critical citizens will spontaneously coalesce into an organization centered around a common purpose. Thus, greater dissatisfaction and more critical evaluations may make the job of would-be organizers easier by reducing organizational costs and providing a more receptive audience, but by no means is organization a costless or automatic product of this dissatisfaction.

Another factor that will likely influence the ability to effectively organize disaffected citizens around a common goal will be the degree to which the citizens of that nation share a collective identity. In countries where there is less sense of a collective identity or where there is historic tension between ethnic, racial, or religious factions within that country, it may be difficult to rally a large enough portion of the population around a common goal, despite the reduced costs of political organization online, to sustain political organization that will compel government recognition or reaction. Smaller groups also become more likely to organize sustained and focused campaigns at less cost. But unless these campaigns can gain leverage either through moving public opinion—either domestic or international—or through some direct influence on power-holding elite, it is not guaranteed that these organizations will effect tangible political change.

A final dimension that will likely determine when and where political evaluations will translate into actual political activity and organization hinges on whether the relevant evaluations are derived from information pertaining to specific events or to more long-term infrastructural problems. While the more systemic, long-term problems are often the most detrimental to good governance compared to discrete events, it will likely be harder to catalyze critical and dissatisfied citizens into activity and organization around these issues. On the other hand, while there is an inertial problem associated with motivating individuals to address entrenched and systemic issues, specific events that dramatically highlight government failures will be more likely to catalyze individuals. Thanks to the immediacy and visibility of these events, they are particularly well-suited to communication through the Internet, which tends to create a sense of urgency and salience. However, it is also likely that public responses to these discrete events may be similarly fleeting and thus unlikely to yield the sustained collective focus and effort to result in real political remedies. In consideration of each of these factors, then, it seems that those instances in which specific and dramatic events communicated online can be effectively linked by would-be organizers to larger systemic issues will likely prove the most successful in creating and maintaining the sustained political activity and organization necessary to actually effect change.

Finally, let's return to the issue of when Internet use will produce evaluations and activities that are prodemocratic in nature and those in which it will produce activity and outcomes that are decidedly undemocratic. As the discussion above suggests, more critical evaluations and greater dissatisfaction alone are unlikely to produce the type of political activity and organization that will effect political change. Instead, although critical evaluations and dissatisfaction lay the necessary foundation, it will still be necessary for a specific catalyst to translate that dissatisfaction into action. These catalysts likely will most often prove to be one or more of the following: specific individual(s) committed to rallying and organizing citizens around a common goal; a specific dramatic event; or the content of discussion online reaching the critical mass necessary to create a collective sense of a specific problem and specific remedy or action to address that problem (which is unlikely to occur without the presence of at least one of the first two types of catalysts listed).

There is simply no guarantee that any of these catalysts will uniformly or automatically favor goals and activities that are prodemocratic in nature. Instead, in some cases, it is perhaps nearly as likely that these catalysts will encourage individuals to express their frustration and dissatisfaction by rallying around decidedly undemocratic actions and goals. This means that these more critical evaluations may, at times, encourage citizens to strive for greater adherence to democratic standards; but in other instances, citizens may be motivated to act toward a clearly undemocratic ends.

After all, democratization tends to be a circuitous and at times rather unpleasant process—likely to produce a considerable degree of angst and uncertainty among citizens from time to time. Thus, there is a question of whether having the missteps and tribulations of democratizing governments projected onto the Internet in real time, shaping evaluations and satisfaction accordingly, will always facilitate the process of democratization. On the one hand, it may expedite the process by providing a mechanism to reveal and document instances of government's failure and thus impel that government to correct its missteps more quickly. It may also spur government action in a democratic direction simply as a result of officials' desire to avoid the activation of the more unruly and unpredictable latent public opinion in the Internet age. On the other hand, critical evaluations and dissatisfaction elicited by exposure to information online may enhance the capacity for individuals or groups (with their own vested interests that are not always prodemocratic) to tap into this angst and leverage dissatisfied citizens toward decidedly undemocratic ends or, at least, to thwart democratic gains.

Time will tell what the full range of the effects of Internet use on political evaluations, satisfaction, behavior, organization, and outcomes will be. But by continuing to identify, unpack, and test the factors that condition the effects of Internet use on political evaluations and satisfaction, researchers can provide useful insight into how this story is likely to unfold. And it is likely that the Internet will end up telling both sides of this story.

NOTES

Chapter One: Why the Effect of Internet Use on Political Evaluations Matters

1. According to Merriam-Webster's Dictionary, a *netizen* is "an active participant in the online community of the Internet."

2. Recent notable exceptions include Howard 2010; Howard & Hussain 2011; Nisbet & Stoycheff 2014; and Nisbet, Stoycheff, & Pearce 2012.

Chapter Two: A Theory of Mirrors and Windows Online

1. This book conforms to definitions provided by Andrew Chadwick (2006) in *Internet Politics* and Bruce Bimber in *Information and American Democracy* (2003). First, the use of the term "Internet" refers to the information environment online rather than the actual technology itself. This is particularly necessary because of the increasing integration of technologies, such as Internet-capable smartphones. Accordingly, I adopt Chadwick's definition of the Internet as "a network of networks of one-to-one, one-to-many, many-to-many, and many-to-one local, national, and global information and communication technologies with relatively open standards and protocols and comparatively low barriers to entry" (2006, 7). I also adopt Bimber's use of the *Oxford English Dictionary* to define "information" as "knowledge communicated concerning some particular fact, subject, or event," which extends beyond facts and does not require any degree of accuracy or veracity. Finally, "communication" is used to denote the transfer or exchange of information in any form.

2. In this context "quality" is not intended to convey some level of intrinsic value belonging to the information. Rather, it simply refers to the type, range, and character of communicated information.

3. This still leaves the issue of media choice, and whether the increasing number of communication channels leads entertainment-seeking audiences to better buffer themselves from news content. This, then, leads to the question of which individuals are more and less likely to consume news online. Each of these potential limitations is discussed in greater detail in chapter 3.

4. Note that this is distinct from *relative deprivation theory*, which argues that social movements and civil strife can be motivated by individuals' sense of relative deprivation. (For an extensive review of the scholarly work in this field, see

Gurney and Tierney 1982.) Whereas relative deprivation theory would suggest that the Internet's window-opening function exposes individuals to the luxuries and better circumstances that individuals in advanced democracies enjoy, thus causing individuals with weak democratic practices to become increasingly dissatisfied—window-opening does not speak to this. Instead, it states that individuals are exposed to more information about how democratic practices function in other countries, particularly advanced democracies that are most visible online, changing the terms through which individuals conceptualize democracy. As a result, government officials lose some degree of control over dictating the criteria their citizens use to evaluate them. Thus, in nations that fall on the lower end of this global metric, evaluations and satisfaction will become more negative. This will happen regardless of whether or not these citizens also acquire a "widespread sense of deprivation" (Gurney & Tierney 1982, 34).

5. Bucy and Gregson (2001) offer such an argument, in which they predict that Internet use will increase satisfaction as a result of enhancing citizens' sense of perceived participation. However, it is important to note that their argument is specific to advanced democracies, and they do not speak to whether any psychic gratification incurred from perceived participation online will automatically apply to citizens in developing and nondemocratic countries.

Chapter Three: Potential Limitations of Mirror-Holding and Window-Opening

1. Yochai Benkler's classic work, *Wealth of Networks,* provides a compelling illustration of the value and necessity of setting appropriate and realistic goalposts for the analyses of communications environments. Rather than setting the expectation of an ideal world of perfect information and then disregarding the effects of information and communication technology when they run up against a realistic set of constraints, acknowledging those constraints and how they condition and limit the effects of technologies within specific communications environments will provide more useful insight into the actual effects of those technologies on the individuals living within those communications environments. As Benkler puts it, "The world we live in is neither a black box nor a cornucopia of well-specified communications channels. However, characterizing the range of possible configurations of the communications environment that we occupy as lying on a spectrum from one end to the other provides us with a framework for describing the degree to which actual conditions of a communications environment are conducive to individual autonomy" (2006, 149).

2. Conversely, "Productive efficiency is concerned with producing goods and services with the optimal combination of inputs to produce maximum output for the minimum cost" (http://www.economicshelp.org/microessays/costs/productive-efficiency/).

3. For a recent review of these literatures, see Mitchelstein and Boczkowski 2010.

4. This assumption is supported by a 2009 Pew Global Attitudes Project survey which found that the Internet is either the first or second preferred source for news for 15% of Russians, 13% of Jordanians, 26% of Palestinians, and 16% of Chinese surveyed.

Chapter Four: Determining the Effect of Internet Use on Democratic (Dis)Satisfaction: The Country Level

1. The data for this indicator were compiled by the United Nations Development Programme and are available at http://hdr.undp.org/en/statistics.

2. Including this single composite measure is preferable to including separate measures of each of these components because these measures are highly collinear, which would invite a degree of instability into the model. However, I also run an additional regression that does include separate measures for each of these three components, which yields congruous findings.

3. The data for this indicator are provided by Reporters Without Borders and are available at http://en.rsf.org/press-freedom-index-2013,1054.html.

4. The data for the World Bank Governance Indicators are available at http://info.worldbank.org/governance/wgi/index.aspx#home.

5. The data for Internet penetration are provided by the International Telecommunication Union and are available at http://www.itu.int/en/ITU-D/Statistics/Pages/stat/default.aspx.

6. A normal probability plot of the studentized residuals confirms that the model's residuals are normally distributed. In addition, plotting the fitted values against the residuals produces a random distribution of points.

Chapter Five: Determining the Effect of Internet Use on Democratic (Dis)Satisfaction: The Individual Level

1. The data for this analysis are provided by the Eurobarometer (Papacostas 2005) and Latinobarometer (2013) organizations.

2. The 1997 data in this analysis are provided by the Eurobarometer (Melich 2007) and Latinobarometer (2013) organizations.

Chapter Seven: At the Internet Café: A Test for Effects in the Tanzanian Election

1. It is worth noting that there are some differences in the methodologies employed in the two field experiments included in this book, which were consequences of more limited funding and stricter time constraints in the Bosnian experiment relative to the later Tanzanian experiment. First, the Tanzanian participants received 75 hours of free Internet time, whereas the Bosnian participants received 60 hours. More importantly, the Tanzanian experiment included a pretest and posttest of both the control and treatment groups. In Bosnia and Herzegovina, due to a limited budget and stricter time constraints, participants in the control group were not given a pretest; however, the treatment group did receive

a pretest. This means that the Tanzanian experiment was a classic pretest-posttest design, whereas the Bosnian experiment conformed more closely to a posttest design. Both of these experimental designs are considered true experiments, capable of testing for a causal relationship, however.

WORKS CITED

Abraham, R. (2007). Mobile phones and economic development: Evidence from the fishing industry in India. *Information Technologies and International Development* 4(1): 5–17.

Aker, J. C. (2008). *Does digital divide or provide? The impact of mobile phones on grain markets in Niger.* BREAD Working Paper No. 177. https://ipl.econ.duke.edu/bread/papers/working/177.pdf.

Alexa. (2013). *Top sites.* Alexa: The Web Information Company. www.alexa.com/topsites.

Almond, G., & Verba, S. (1963). *The civic culture: Political attitudes and democracy in five nations.* Princeton, NJ: Princeton University Press.

Almond, M. (2011, Feb. 13). Egypt unrest. *BBC News Middle East.* http://www.bbc.co.uk/news/world-middle-east-12431231.

Althaus, S. L., & Tewksbury, D. (2002). Agenda setting and the "new" news: Patterns of issue importance among readers of the paper and online versions of the *New York Times. Communications Research* 29: 180–207.

Ambah, F. S. (2006, Nov. 12). New clicks in the Arab world: Bloggers challenge longtime cultural, political restrictions. *Washington Post,* A13.

Amos, D. (2011, Sept. 25). Pro-Assad "army" wages cyberwar in Syria. NPR. http://www.npr.org/2011/09/25/140746510/pro-assad-army-wages-cyberwar-in-syria.

Amrani, I. E. (2011, Jan.–Feb.). Three decades of a joke that just won't die. *Foreign Policy.* http://www.foreignpolicy.com/articles/2011/01/02/three_decades_of_a_joke_that_just_wont_die?page=0,1&wp_login_redirect=0.

Anderson, C. J., & Guillory, C. A. (1997). Political institutions and satisfaction with democracy: A cross-national analysis of consensus and majoritarian systems. *American Political Science Review* 91(1): 66–81.

Annan, K. (1997, June 22). Address to the World Bank conference "Global Knowledge '97," Toronto, Canada.

Associated Press. (2011, Sept. 27). Chaves says adios to critics—in 140 characters. *Fox News.* http://www.foxnews.com/tech/2011/09/27/hackers-hijack-twitter-accounts-chavez-critics.

Bailard, C. S. (2009). Mobile phone diffusion and corruption in Africa. *Political Communication* 26(3): 333–353.

Baltagi, B. (2008). *Econometric analysis of panel data.* Hoboken, NJ: John Wiley & Sons.

Bamman, D., O'Connor, B., & Smith, N. A. (2012, Mar. 5). Censorship and deletion practices in Chinese social media. *First Monday* 17(3). http://firstmonday
.org/ htbin/cgiwrap/bin/ojs/index.php/fm/article/view/3943/3169.

Barboza, D. (2011, Jan. 30). Chinese man who bragged of privilege gets six years.
New York Times. http://www.nytimes.com/2011/01/31/world/asia/31china.html?
_r=0.

Baum, M. (2003). *Soft news goes to war: Public opinion and American foreign
policy in the new media age.* Princeton, NJ: Princeton University Press.

Baviskar, S., &. Malone, M. F. T. (2004). What democracy means to citizens—and
why it matters. *Revista Europea de Estudios Latinoamericanos y del Caribe* 76:
3–23.

BBC. (2010, Mar.). BBC's international news services attract record global audience despite short wave radio losses of 20 million. *BBC World Service Publicity.*

BBC News. (2004, Nov. 15). Election apology starts new feud. http://news.bbc.co
.uk/2/hi/technology/4012621.stm.

Benkler, Y. (2006). *The wealth of networks: How social production transforms
markets and freedom.* New Haven, CT: Yale University Press.

Bennett, D. (2013, Aug. 21). The visual evidence of a chemical attack in Syria is
overwhelming and disturbing. *Atlantic Wire.* http://www.theatlanticwire.com/
global/2013/08/visual-evidence-syrias-poison-gas-attack-overwhelming-and-
disturbing/68586.

Bennett, W. L. (2007, Mar. 5–6). Changing citizenship in the digital age. Paper presented at Millennial Learners conference, Florence. http://www.oecd.org/edu/
ceri/38360794.pdf.

Bennett, W. L., & Manheim, J. (2006, Nov.). The one-step flow of communication.
ANNALS of the American Academy of Political and Social Science 608(1):
213–232. doi: 10.1177/0002716206292266.

Bernal, V. (2006). Diaspora, cyberspace, and political imagination: The Eritrean
diaspora online. *Global Networks* 6(2): 161–179.

Best, M. L., & Wade, K. W. (2009). The Internet and democracy: Global catalyst
or democratic dud? *Bulletin of Science, Technology & Society* 29: 255–271.
doi: 10.1177/0270467609336304.

Bimber, B. (1998). The Internet and political transformation: Populism, community, and accelerated pluralism. *Polity* 31: 133–160.

Bimber, B. (2001). Information and political engagement in America: The search
for effects of information technology at the individual level. *Political Research
Quarterly* 54: 53–67.

Bimber, B. (2003). *Information and American democracy: Technology in the evolution of political power.* Cambridge, MA: Cambridge University Press

Bockowski, P., & de Santos, M. (2007). When more media equals less news: Patterns of content homogenization in Argentina's leading print and online newspapers. *Political Communication* 24(2): 167–180.

Boulianne, S. (2009). Does Internet use affect engagement? A meta-analysis of research. *Political Communication* 26(2): 193–211.

Bratton, M., & Mattes, R. (2001). Support for democracy in Africa: Intrinsic or instrumental? *British Journal of Political Science* 31: 447–474.

Briggs, A., & Burke, P. (2009). *A social history of the media: From Gutenberg to the Internet*. Malden, MA: Polity Press.

Broadcasting Board of Governors. (2013). Voice of America. http://www.bbg.gov/broadcasters/voa.

Bucy, E. P., & Gregson, K. S. (2001). Media participation: A legitimizing mechanism of mass democracy. *New Media & Society* 3(3): 357–380.

Cass, S. (2007, May 29). How much does the Internet weigh? *Discover Magazine*. http://discovermagazine.com/2007/jun/how-much-does-theinternetweigh/?searchterm=weight %20internet.

Castells, M. (2011). *The rise of the network society: Vol. 1. The information age: Economy, society, and culture*. Oxford: Blackwell.

CBS News. (2011, Apr. 13). Six-year-old's pat down at airport sparks outrage. http://www.cbsnews.com/news/six-year-olds-patdown-at-airport-sparks-outrage/

Central Intelligence Agency. (2008). *The CIA world factbook 2009*. New York: Skyhorse Publishing Inc.

Chadwick, A. (2006). *Internet politics: States, citizens, and new communication technologies*. New York: Oxford University Press.

Chalbi, Mona. (2013, Sept. 3). Syrian electronic army's war on the web: Interactive timeline. *The Guardian*. http://www.theguardian.com/world/interactive/2013/sep/03/syrian-electronic-army-war-web-timeline.

Chang, J. (2003). *Wild swans: Three daughters of China*. New York: Simon & Schuster.

Chappell, B. (2013, Sept. 29). Remarks on women's ovaries exposes Saudi cleric to ridicule. NPR. http://www.npr.org/blogs/thetwo-way/2013/09/29/227461004/remarks-on-womens-ovaries-expose-saudi-cleric-to-ridicule.

Chick, K. (2010, June 18). Beating death of Egyptian businessman Khalid Said spotlights police brutality. *Christian Science Monitor*. http://www.csmonitor.com/World/Middle-East/2010/0618/Beating-death-of-Egyptian-businessman-Khalid-Said-spotlights-police-brutality.

China Digital Times. (2010). Latest directives from the Ministry of Truth, October 22–November 7, 2010. Retrieved from: http://chinadigitaltimes.net/2010/11/latest-directives-from-the-ministry-of-truth-october-22-november-7-2010.

Christenson, K., & Levinson, D. (eds.). (2003). *Encyclopedia of community: From the village to the virtual world* (Vol. 2). Thousand Oaks, CA: Sage Publications.

CIC. (2008). *A special edition of the guide to Internet word of mouth: Internet and IWOM shape the Sichuan earthquake aftermath*. http://www.slideshare.net/CIC_China/iwom-watch-may-special-edition.

Cisco. (2011, June 1). *Cisco visual networking index: Forecast and methodology, 2010–2015.* White Paper. http://www.cisco.com/en/US/solutions/collateral/ns341/ns525/ns537/ns705/ns827/white_paper_c11–481360.pdf.

Clarke, H. D., Dutt, N., & Kornberg, A. (1993). The political economy of attitudes toward polity and society in western European democracies. *Journal of Politics* 55: 998–1021.

Coleman, R., & McCombs, M. (2007). The young and agenda-less? Exploring age-related differences in agenda setting on the youngest generation, baby boomers, and the civic generation. *Journalism & Mass Communication Quarterly* 84(3): 495–508.

Conaway, S. (2013). The great firewall: How China polices Internet traffic. *Certification.* http://www.certmag.com/read.php?in=3906

Curtis, A. (2011). A brief history of the World Wide Web. http://www2.uncp.edu/home/acurtis/Courses/ResourcesForCourses/WebHistory.html.

Dahlgren, P. (2005). The Internet, public spheres, and political communication: Dispersion and deliberation. *Political Communications* 22: 147–162.

Dalton, R. J., Shin, D. C., & Willy, J. (2007). *Popular conceptions of the meaning of democracy: Democratic understanding in unlikely places.* Center for the Study of Democracy, University of California, Irvine. http://repositories.cdlib.org/csd/07–03.

Davies, J. C. (1997). *When men revolt and why.* New Brunswick, NJ: Transaction Publishers.

Davis, R. (1999). *The Web of politics: The Internet's impact on the American political system.* New York: Oxford University Press.

Denters, B., Gabriel, O., & Torcal, M. (2007). Political confidence in representative democracies: Socio-cultural vs. political explanations. In J. W. Van Deth, J. R. Montero, & A. Westholm (eds.), *Citizenship and involvement in European democracies: A comparative analysis,* 66–87. New York: Routledge.

Diamond, L. (2008). *The spirit of democracy: The struggle to build free societies throughout the world.* New York: Holt Paperbacks.

Diamond, L., & Plattner, M. F. (eds.). (2012). *Liberation technology: Social media and the struggle for democracy.* Baltimore: Johns Hopkins University Press.

Donner, J. (2005). The mobile behaviors of Kigali's microentrepreneurs: Whom they call . . . And why. In K. Nyiri (ed.), *A sense of place: The global and the local in mobile communication.* Vienna: Passagen.

Donner, J. (2006). The social and economic implications of mobile telephony in Rwanda: An ownership/access typology. *Knowledge, Technology, & Policy* 19(2): 17–28.

Earl, J., & Kimport, K. (2011). *Digitally enabled social change: Activism in the Internet age.* Cambridge, MA: MIT Press.

Entman, R. M. (2003a). Cascading activation: Contesting the White House's frame after 9/11. *Political Communication* 20: 415–433.

Entman, R. M. (2003b). *Projections of power: Framing news, public opinion, and U.S. foreign policy.* Chicago: University of Chicago Press.

Essounggou, A. (2010, Dec.). A social media boom begins in Africa. *Africa Renewal.*

European Stability Initiative. (2004). Governance and democracy in Bosnia and Herzegovina: Post-industrial society and the authoritarian temptation. United Kingdom Department for International Development. www.esiweb.org.

Evans, G., & Whitefield, S. (1995). The politics and economics of democratic commitment: Support for democracy in transition societies. *British Journal of Politics* 25: 485–514.

Farnsworth, S., & Owen, D. (2004). Internet use and the 2000 presidential election. *Electoral Studies* 23: 415–429.

Fiorina, M. P. (1978). Economic retrospective voting in American national elections: A micro-analysis. *American Journal of Political Science,* 22(2), 426–443.

Franklin, C. H. (1989). Estimation across data sets: Two-stage auxiliary instrumental variables estimation (2SAIV). *Political Analysis* 1(1): 1–23.

Freedom House. (2003). *Nations in transit: Bosnia and Herzegovina.* http://www .freedomhouse.org/report/nations-transit/2003/bosnia-and-herzegovina#. UwzmZM4wA00.

Freedom House. (2010). *Map of press freedom 2010.* http://www.freedomhouse .org/sites/default/files/MOPF2010—final.pdf.

Freedom House. (2011). *Freedom on the Net: China.* http://www.freedomhouse .org/images/File/FotN/China2011.pdf.

Freedom House (2012). *Methodology: Freedom in the world 2012.* http://www .freedomhouse.org/report/freedom-world-2012/methodology#.UwzX3M4 wA00.

Frontline. (2011, Feb. 22). *Revolution in Cairo: How it started.* Public Broadcasting Service. http://www.pbs.org/wgbh/pages/frontline/revolution-in-cairo/ inside-april6-movement.

Frost & Sullivan. (2006). *Social impact of mobile telephony in Latin America.* GSM LatinAmerica.http://www.gsm.org/documents/Social_Impact_of_Mobile_Tele phonyin_Latin_America.pdf.

Gentzkow, M., & Shapiro, J. M. (2011). Ideological segregation online and offline. *Quarterly Journal of Economics* 126(4): 1799–1839.

Global Voices. (2010, Oct. 25). "My father is Li Gang" goes viral in China. *The Castlegar Source.* castlegarsource.com/news/my-father-li-gang-goes-viral-china

Graber, D. A. (1997). *Mass media and American politics,* 5th ed. Washington, DC: Congressional Quarterly Press.

Greengard, M. (2011). *The other Russia.* http://www.theotherrussia.org/about.

Gurney, J. N., & Tierney, K. J. (1982). Relative deprivation and social movements: A critical look at twenty years of theory and research. *Sociological Quarterly* 23(1): 33–47.

Habermas, J. (1991). *The structural transformation of the public sphere: An inquiry into a category of bourgeois society.* Cambridge, MA: MIT Press.

Harmel, R., & Robertson, J. D. (1986). Government stability and regime support: A cross-national analysis. *Journal of Politics* 48: 1029–1040.

Hastie, R., & Park, B. (1986). The relationship between memory and judgment depends on whether the judgment task is memory-based or on-line. *Psychological Review* 93(3): 258–268.

Hetherington, M. J. (1998). The political relevance of political trust. *American Political Science Review* 92(4): 791–808.

Hiltz, S. R., & Turoff, M. (1985). Structuring computer mediated communication systems to avoid information overload. *Communication of the ACM* 28: 680–689.

Hindman, M. S. (2009). *The myth of digital democracy*. Princeton, NJ: Princeton University Press.

Holst, C. (2003). The validity of income measurements in comparative perspective. In J. H. P. Hoffmeyer-Zlotnik & C. Wolf (eds.), *Advances in cross-national comparison: A European working book for demographic and socio-economic variables*. New York: Kluwer Academic / Plenum.

Horrigan, J. B. (2006, Mar. 22). *Online news*. Pew Internet & American Life Project and University of Michigan School of Information. http://www.per internet.org.

Horrigan, J., Garrett, K., & Resnick, P. (2004). *The Internet and democratic debate*. Pew Internet and American Life Project and the University of Michigan School of Information. http://www.pewinternet.org/~/media/Files/Reports/2004/PIP_Political_Info_Report.pdf.

Howard, P. N. (2010). *The digital origins of dictatorship and democracy*. New York: Oxford University Press.

Howard, P. N., & Hussain, M. M. (2011). The upheavals in Egypt and Tunisia: The role of digital media. *Journal of Democracy* 22(3): 35–48.

Huntington, Samuel. (1993). *The third wave*. Norman: University of Oklahoma Press.

Inglehart, R., & Welzel, C. (2005). *Modernization, cultural change, and democracy: The Human development sequence*. New York: Cambridge University Press.

International Business Times. (2011, May 27). *North Korea's Happiness Index rank: China top, US bottom*. http://sanfrancisco.ibtimes.com/articles/153551/20110527/north-korea-happiness-index-rank-china-top-us-bottom-photos.htm.

International Telecommunications Union: ICT Eye. (2008). *Country reports: Bosnia & Herzegovina*. http://www.itu.int/ITU-D/icteye/DisplayCountry.aspx?countryId=275.

International Telecommunications Union (ITU). (2013). *The world in 2013: ICT facts and figures*. http://www.itu.int/en/ITUD/Statistics/Documents/facts/ICT FactsFigures2013.pdf.

Internet World Stats. (2012). *Facebook users in the world: Facebook usage and*

Facebook growth statistics by world geographic regions. http://www.internet worldstats.com/facebook.htm.

Internet World Stats. (2013). *Internet users in the world.* http://www.internetworld stats.com/stats.htm.

Internews Center for Innovation and Learning. (2012, July). *Mapping the maps: A meta-level analysis of Ushahidi and Crowdmap.* http://irevolution.files.word press.com/2013/01/internewswpcrowdglobe_web-1.pdf.

Iyengar, S. (1990). The accessibility bias in politics: Television news and public opinion. *International Journal of Public Opinion Research* 2: 1–15.

Iyengar, S. (1994). *Is anyone responsible? How television frames political issues.* Chicago: University of Chicago Press.

Iyengar, S., & Kinder, D. R. (1987). *News that matters: Television and American opinion.* Chicago: University of Chicago Press.

Jamjoom, M. (2013a, Sept. 29). Saudi cleric warns driving could damage women's ovaries. CNN. http://www.cnn.com/2013/09/29/world/meast/saudi-arabia-women-driving-cleric/index.html.

Jamjoom, M. (2013b, Sept. 26). Saudi women's new campaign to end driving ban. CNN. http://www.cnn.com/2013/09/26/world/meast/saudi-arabia-women-drivers/index.html.

Jeffries, I. (2011). *Political developments in contemporary China: A guide.* New York: Routledge.

Jensen, R. (2007). The digital provide: Information (technology), market performance, and welfare in the South Indian fisheries sector. *Quarterly Journal of Economics* 122(3): 879–924.

Johnson, T. J., & Barbara, K. K. (2003). A boost or bust for democracy? How the Web influenced political attitudes and behaviors in the 1996 and 2000 presidential elections. *Press/Politics* 8: 9–34. doi: 10.1177/1081180X03008003002.

Kalathil, S., & Boas, T. C. (2001). *The Internet and state control in authoritarian regimes: China, Cuba, and the counter-revolution.* Washington, DC: Carnegie Endowment for International Peace. http://www.carnegieendowment.org/publications/index.cfm?fa=view&id=728.

Kalathil, S., & Boas, T. C. (2003). *Open networks, closed regimes.* Washington, DC: Carnegie Endowment for International Peace. http://www.asu.edu/courses /pos445/Open%20Networks%20Closed%20Regimes.pdf.

Karam, Z. (2011, Sept. 27). Syria wages cyber warfare as websites hacked. *Washington Times.* http://www.washingtontimes.com/news/2011/sep/27/syria-wages-cyber-warfare-as-websites-hacked/?page=all.

Kasparov, G. (2007, June 4). Putin's critics, a Web strategy: We are banned from TV, so activists put videos of rallies on YouTube. *Business Week* 4037: 112.

Katz, E., Gurevitch, M., & Haas, H. (1973). On the use of the mass media for important things. *American Sociological Review* 38: 164–181.

Katz, E., & Lazarsfeld, P. F. (1955). *Personal influence: The part played by people in the flow of mass communications.* New York: Free Press.

Kedzie, C. (1997). *Communication and democracy: Coincident revolutions and the emergent dictators.* Santa Monica, CA: RAND. http://www.rand.org/pubs/rgs_dissertations/RGSD127.

Kenski, K., & Stroud, N. J. (2006). Connections between Internet use and political efficacy, knowledge, & participation. *Journal of Broadcasting and Electronic Media* 5(2): 173–192.

Key, V. O. (1961). *Public opinion and American democracy.* New York: Alfred A. Knopf.

Kinder, D., & Kiewiet, R. (1981, Apr.). Sociotropic politics: The American case. *British Journal of Political Science* 11: 129–161. doi: 10.1017/S00071234 00002544.

King, G., Pan, J., & Roberts, M. (2013). How censorship in China allows government criticism but silences collective expression. *American Political Science Review.* 107(2): 326–343.

Kleinberg, J., & Lawrence, S. (2001). The structure of the Web. *Science* 294: 1849–1850.

Know Your Meme (2011). *My Dad is Li Gang!* http://knowyourmeme.com/memes/events/my-dad-is-li-gang %E6%88%91%E7%88%B8%E6%98%AF %E6%9D%8E%E5%88%9A.

Kornberg, A., & Clarke, H. D. (1994, Sept.). Beliefs about democracy and satisfaction with democratic government: The Canadian case. *Political Research Quarterly* 47(3): 537–563. doi: 10.1177/106591299404700301.

Kricheli, R., Livne, Y., & Magaloni, B. (2011, Apr. 15). *Taking to the streets: Theory and evidence on protests under authoritarianism.* APSA 2010 Annual Meeting Paper. Available at SSRN: http://ssrn.com/abstract=1642040.

Kwak, N., Poor, N., & Skoric, M. M. (2006). Honey, I shrunk the world! The relation between Internet use and international engagement. *Mass Communication and Society* 9(2): 189–213.

Lane, B., Sweet, S., Lewin, D., Sephton, J., & Petini, I. (2006, Apr.). *The economic and social benefits of mobile services in Bangladesh: A case study for the GSM Association.* London: Ovum.

Latinobarometer. (2013). *Data bank.* Latinobarometro Corporation. http://www.latinobarometro.org/latino/LATDatos.jsp.

Lau, M. (2005). Internet development and information control in the People's Republic of China. *CRS Report for Congress.* http://www.au.af.mil/au/awc/awcgate/crs/rl33167.pdf.

Lawrence, D. (2008, Nov. 17). China substitutes "spin" for suppression as Web weakens control. *Bloomberg.* http://www.bloomberg.com/apps/news?pid=news archive&sid=amFtFkI.V7nI&refer=news.

Lee, J. K. (2009). Incidental exposure to news: Limiting fragmentation in the new media environment. Ph.D. diss., University of Texas at Austin. http://repositories.lib.utexas.edu.

Levitsky, S., & Way, L. (2002). The rise of competitive authoritarianism. *Journal of Democracy* 13(2): 51–65. doi: 10.1353/jod.2002.0026.

Lipmann, W. (1922). *Public opinion.* New York: Free Press.

Livingston, S. (2011). *Africa's evolving infosystems: A pathway to security and stability.* Africa Center for Strategic Studies Research Paper No. 2.

Lodge, M., McGraw, K. M., & Stroh, P. (1989). An impression-driven model of candidate evaluation. *American Political Science Review* 83(2): 399–419.

Lohmann, S. (1993). A Signaling model of informative and manipulative political action. *American Political Science Review* 87(2): 319–333.

Low, A. (2006, Nov. 10). Singapore: Relax rules on traditional media for open political debate. *UCLA International Institute, Straits Times.* http://www.international.ucla.edu/article.asp?parentid=57497.

Lum, T. (2006). *Internet development and information control in the People's Republic of China.* CRS Report RL33167. Washington, DC: Congressional Research Service, Library of Congress.

Lyman, P., & Varian, H. R. (2000). *How much information.* University of California at Berkeley. http://www.sims.berkeley.edu/how-much-info.

Lynch, M. (2011). After Egypt: The limits and promise of online challenges to the authoritarian Arab state. *Perspectives on Politics* 9(2): 301–310. doi: 10.1017/S1537592711000910.

Lynch, M., Glasser, S. B., & Hounshell, B. (eds.). (2011). Revolution in the Arab world: Tunisia, Egypt, and the unmaking of an era. In *Foreign Policy.* Washington, DC: Slate Group.

Maier, S. (2010). All the news fit to post? Comparing news content on the Web to newspapers, television, and radio. *Journalism Mass Communication Quarterly* 87(3–4): 548–562.

Melich, A. (1997, Mar.–Apr.). *Eurobarometer 47.1: Images of Switzerland, education throughout life, racism, and patterns of family planning and work status* [Computer file]. Conducted by INRA (Europe), Brussels, on request of the European Commission. ZA 1st ed. Cologne, Germany: Zentralarchiv für Empirische Sozialforschung [producer and distributor], 2000. Ann Arbor, MI: Inter-university Consortium for Political and Social Research [distributor], 2000.

Miller, A. H., Hesli, V. L., & Reisinger, W. M. (1997, Apr.). Conceptions of democracy among mass and elite in post-Soviet societies. *British Journal of Political Science* 27: 157–190.

Milner, H. (2006, Mar.). The digital divide: The role of political institutions in technology diffusion. *Comparative Political Studies* 39(2): 176–199. doi: 10.1177/0010414005282983.

Mishler, W., & Rose, R. (2005). What are the political consequences of trust? A test of cultural and institutional theories in Russia. *Comparative Political Studies* 20(10): 1–29. doi: 10.1177/0010414005278419.

Mitchelstein, E., & Boczkowski, P. J. (2010). Online news consumption research: An assessment of past work and an agenda for the future. *New Media & Society* 12(7): 1085–1102.

Moehler, D. C. (2008). *Distrusting Democrats: Outcomes of participatory constitution making*. Ann Arbor: University of Michigan Press.

Molony, T. S. J. (2005). *Food, carvings and shelter: The adoption and appropriation of information and communication technologies in Tanzanian micro and small enterprises*. Ph.D. diss., University of Edinburgh.

Morozov, E. (2011a). *The Net delusion: The dark side of Internet freedom*. New York: Public Affairs.

Morozov, E. (2011b). How the Kremlin harnesses the Internet. *New York Times*. http://www.nytimes.com/2011/01/05/opinion/05iht-edmorozov04.html?_r=0.

Mossberger, K., Kaplan, D., & Gilbert, M. (2008). Going online without easy access: A tale of three cities. *Journal of Urban Affairs* 30(5): 469–488.

Mossberger, K., & Tolbert, C. J. (2010). Digital democracy: How politics online is changing electoral participation. In J. E. Leighley (ed.), *The Oxford handbook of American elections and political behavior*. Oxford: Oxford University Press.

Mossberger, K., Tolbert, C. J., & McNeal, R. S. (2008). *Digital citizenship: The Internet, society, and participation*. Cambridge, MA: MIT Press.

Mydans, S. (2011, May 5). In Singapore, political campaigning goes viral. *New York Times*. http://www.nytimes.com/2011/05/06/world/asia/06iht-singapore06.html.

Naughton, J. (2006, Nov. 16). How the bloggers of Iran are keeping Iranian freedoms alive. *The Observer*. http://www.guardian.co.uk/media/2006/nov/19/business.newmedia.

Nielson, J. (1995). *Multimedia and hypertext: The Internet and beyond*. San Diego, CA: Academic Press.

Nisbet, E., & Stoycheff, E. (2014). What's the bandwidth for democracy? Deconstructing Internet penetration and citizen attitudes about governance. *Political Communication* (forthcoming).

Nisbet, E. C., Stoycheff, E., & Pearce, K. E. (2012). Internet use and democratic demands: A multinational, multilevel model of Internet use and citizen attitudes about democracy. *Journal of Communication* 62(2): 249–265.

Norris, P. (2001). *A digital divide: Civic engagement, information poverty, and the Internet in democratic societies*. New York: Cambridge University Press.

Papacostas, Antonis. (2005, May–June). *Eurobarometer 63.4: European Union enlargement, the European constitution, economic challenges, innovative products and services* [Computer file]. ICPSR04564-v2. Conducted by TNS Opinion & Social, Brussels, Belgium. ZA ed. Cologne, Germany: Zentralarchiv fur Empirische Sozialforschung [producer], 2007. Cologne, Germany: Zentralarchiv fur Empirische Sozialforschung/Ann Arbor, MI: Inter-university Consortium for Political and Social Research [distributors], 2008-10-03. doi: 10.3886/ICPSR04564.

Pasek, J., Kenski, K., Romer, D., & Jamieson, K. H. (2006). America's youth and community engagement: How use of the mass media is related to civic activity and political awareness in 14- to 22-year olds. *Communication Research* 33(3): 115–135.

Patai, R. (2002). *The Arab mind*. New York: Hatherleigh Press.

Patterson, T. E. (1994). *Out of order: An incisive and boldly original critique of the news media's domination of America's political process*. New York: Knopf Doubleday.

Pawlowski, A. (2011, June 8). *Soldiers' $2,800 in bag fees spark outrage, policy change*. CNN. http://www.cnn.com/2011/TRAVEL/06/08/soldiers.bags.delta.

Pearce, N. (2000). The ecological fallacy strikes back. *Journal of Epidemiology and Community Health* 54(5): 326–327.

Pew Research Center. (2010, Sept. 12). *Americans spending more time following the news*. http://www.people-press.org/2010/09/12/americans-spending-more-time-following-the-news.

Pew Research Center for the People and the Press. (2004, June 8). *Online news audience larger, more diverse: News audiences increasingly politicized*. http://www.people-press.org/files/legacy-pdf/215.pdf.

Pew Research Global Attitudes Project. (2009). *Spring 2009 survey data: 25-nation survey conducted May 18–June 16, 2009*. http://www.pewglobal.org/2009/06/16/spring-2009-survey-data.

Preston, J. (2011). Movement began with outrage and a Facebook page that gave it an outlet. *New York Times*. http://www.nytimes.com/2011/02/06/world/middleeast/06face.html?pagewanted=1&_r=2.

Prior, M. (2005). News vs. entertainment: How increasing media choice widens gaps in political knowledge and turnout. *American Journal of Political Science* 49(3): 577–592.

Purcell, K., Rainie, L., Mitchell, A., Rosenstiel, T., & Olmstead, K. (2010, Mar.). *Understanding the participatory news consumer: How Internet and cell phone users have turned news into a social experience*. Pew Internet & American Life Project. http://infousa.state.gov/media/internet/docs/participatory-news-consumer.pdf.

Reporters Without Borders (2010). *Press Freedom Index 2010*. http://en.rsf.org/press-freedom-index-2010,1034.html.

Reporters Without Borders. (2011, Mar. 11). *Internet enemies: Cuba*. http://en.rsf.org/internet-enemie-cuba,39756.html.

Richards, D. L. (2002). Making the national international: Information technology and government respect for human rights. In J. E. Allison (ed.), *Technology, development, and democracy: International conflict and cooperation in the information age*, 105–130. Albany: State University of New York Press.

Rigg, J. (2012, Nov. 16). *Sina Weibo exceeds 400 million users, sees increasing mobile traffic*. Engadget. http://www.engadget.com/2012/11/16/sina-weibo-400-million-users.

Samuel, J., Shah, N., & Hadingham, W. (2005). *Mobile communications in South*

Africa, Tanzania, and Egypt: Results from community and business surveys in Africa; The economic impact of mobile phones. Vodafone Policy Paper Series No. 3.

Sarsfield, R., & Echegary, F. (2006). Democracy and its perceived efficacy affect regime preference in Latin America. *International Journal of Public Opinion* 18(2): 153–173. doi: 10.1093/ijpor/edh088.

Scheufele, D. A., & Nisbet, M. C. (2002). Being a citizen online: New opportunities and dead ends. *Press/Politics* 7(3): 55–75.

Schudson, M. (2004). Click here for democracy: A History and critique of an information-based model of citizenship. In H. Jenkins & D. Thorburn (eds.), *Democracy and new media.* Cambridge, MA: MIT Press.

Shirky, C. (2009). *Here comes everybody: The power of organizing without organizations.* New York: Penguin Group.

60 Minutes. (2011, Feb. 16). Wael Ghonim and Egypt's new age revolution. *CBS News.* http://www.cbsnews.com/8301–18560_162–20031701/wael-ghonim-and-egypts-new-age-revolution.

Slackman, M. (2011, Mar. 17). Bullets stall youthful push for Arab Spring. *New York Times.* http://www.nytimes.com/2011/03/18/world/middleeast/18youth.html?pagewanted=all.

Smith, A. (2010). *Government online.* Pew Research Internet Project. http://www.pewinternet.org/2010/04/27/government-online.

Speigel, B. (2011, Nov. 19). From safety of New York, reporting on distant home. *New York Times.* http://www.nytimes.com/2011/11/20/nyregion/from-safety-of-new-york-reporting-on-a-distant-homeland.html?pagewanted=all&_r=0.

Stelter, B. (2011, Jan. 31). Al Jazeera English finds an audience. *New York Times.*

Stiglitz, J. (2002). Transparency in government [Free PDF]. In Islam, R. (ed.), *The right to tell: The role of mass media in economic development.* Washington, DC: World Bank.

Stimson, J. A. (1985). Regression in space and time: A statistical essay. *American Journal of Political Science* 29(4): 914–947.

Stroud, N. J. (2008). Media use and political predispositions: Revisiting the concept of selective exposure. *Political Behavior* 30(3): 341–366.

Sullivan, J. (2012). A tale of two microblogs in China. *Media, Culture & Society* 34: 773–783. doi: 10.1177/0163443712448951.

Sunstein, C. R. (2001). *Republic.com.* Princeton, NJ: Princeton University Press.

Sydell, L. (2008). *Chinese fans follow American TV online—for free.* NPR. http://www.npr.org/templates/story/story.php?storyId=91799790.

Tam, D. (2013, Jan. 30). *Facebook by the numbers: 1.06 billion monthly active users.* CNet. http://news.cnet.com/8301–1023_3–57566550–93/facebook-by-the-numbers-1.06-billion-monthly-active-users.

Tanzania Election Monitoring Committee (TEMCO). (2010). *An interim report on performance of Tanzania's 2010 general election in Tanzania.* http://www.tz

.undp.org/ESP/docs/Observer_Reports/TEMCO_interim_report_UnionElec
tions2010.pdf.

Tewksbury, D. (2005). The seeds of audience fragmentation: Specialization in the
use of online news sites. *Journal of Broadcasting & Electronic Media* 49(3):
332–348.

Tewksbury, D., & Althaus, S. L. (2000). Differences in knowledge acquisition
among readers of the paper and online versions of a national newspaper. *Journalism & Mass Communication Quarterly* 77: 457–479.

Tewksbury, D., & Rittenberg, J. (2009). Online news creation and consumption:
Implications for modern democracies. In A. Chadwick & P. N. Howard (eds.),
Routledge handbook of Internet politics, 186–200. New York: Routledge.

Tewksbury, D., Weaver, A. J., & Maddex, B. D. (2001). Accidentally informed:
News exposure on the World Wide Web. *Journalism and Mass Communication Quarterly* 78(3): 533–554.

Tolbert, C. J., & McNeal, R. S. (2003). Unraveling the effect of the Internet on political participation. *Political Research Quarterly* 56: 175–185. doi: 10.1177/
106591290305600206.

Tolbert, C. J., & Mossberger, K. (2006). The effects of e-government on trust and
confidence in government. *Public Administration Review* 66(3): 354–369. doi:
10.1111/j.1540-6210.2006.00594.

Tufekci, Z., & Wilson, C. (2012). Social media and the decision to participate in
political protest: Observations from Tahrir Square. *Journal of Communication* 62(2): 363–379.

Tyler, P. E. (1995, Jan. 28). Tangshan journal: After eating bitterness, 100 flowers
blossom. *New York Times.* http://www.nytimes.com/1995/01/28/world/tang
shan-journal-after-eating-bitterness-100-flowers-blossom.html.

UNESCO. (2005). Towards knowledge societies. *UNESCO World Report.* http://
unesdoc.unesco.org/images/0014/001418/141843e.pdf.

Universal Declaration of Human Rights. http://www.un.org/en/documents/udhr/
index.shtml.

Want China Times. (2011, Mar. 15). Netizens admire Japanese response to disaster. http://www.wantchinatimes.com/news-subclass-cnt.aspx?id=2011031500
0175&cid=1103.

Wauters, R. (2010, Jan. 19). Report: Skype now accounts for 12% of all international calling minutes. *TechCrunch.* http://techcrunch.com/2010/01/19/skype-
international-calling-minutes-share.

Webster, J. G., & Ksiazek, T. B. (2012). The dynamics of audience fragmentation:
Public attention in an age of digital media. *Journal of Communication* 62(1):
39–56.

Welch, E. W., Hinnant, C. C., & Moon, M. J. (2005). Linking citizen satisfaction
with e-government and trust in government. *Journal of Public Administration
Research and Theory* 15(3): 371–391.

West, D. M. (2007). Global e-government, 2007. *Inside Politics.* http://www.inside politics.org/egovt07int.pdf.

White, R. K. (1949, Apr.). Hitler, Roosevelt, and the nature of war propaganda. *Journal of Abnormal and Social Psychology* 44(2): 157–174. doi: 10.1037/h0056667.

Whitton, J. B. (1951). Cold war propaganda. *American Journal of International Law* 45(1): 151–153.

Williams, C. (2011, Jan. 5). US gov funds censorship-busting tech alternatives to Wikileaks: How about some Chinese or Iranian secrets for a change? *The Register.* http://www.theregister.co.uk/2011/01/05/censorship_grants_wikileaks.

World Bank. (2011). Governance matters III: Frequently asked questions. *Governance & Anti-Corruption.* http://web.worldbank.org/WBSITE/EXTERNAL/WBI/EXTWBIGOVANTCOR/0,,contentMDK:20964853~menuP-K:1976990~pagePK:64168445~piPK:64168309~theSitePK:1740530~is-CURL:Y,00.html.

Xenos, M., & Moy, P. (2007). Direct and differential effects of the Internet on political and civic engagement. *Journal of Communication* 57(4): 704–718. doi: 10.1111/j.1460–2466.2007.00364.

Zaller, J. (2003). Coming to grips with V. O. Key's concept of latent opinion. In M. B. MacKuen & G. Rabinowitz (eds.), *Electoral democracy*, 311–336. Ann Arbor: University of Michigan Press.

Zillmann, D., & Bryant, J. (1985). *Selective exposure to communication.* Mahwah, NJ: Lawrence Erlbaum Associates.

Zmerli, S., Newton, K., & Montero, J. R. (2007). Trust in people, confidence in political institutions, and satisfaction with democracy. In J. W. Van Deth, J. R. Montero, & A. Westholm (eds.), *Citizenship and involvement in European democracies,* 35–65. New York: Routledge.

quality of life, democratic satisfaction and, 130–31

radio, 25
random effects models, 70–71
regression models, 69–70
relative deprivation theory, 139–40n4
Religious Meditations, of Heresies (Bacon), 24
representative democracies, 2
revolution, likelihood of, 132
rich-get-richer phenomenon, 46
Russia: government of, cyber warfare by, 53–54; state-sponsored propaganda in, 55

Said, Khaled, 11–12, 14
satisfaction, Internet's effect on, 19–20 (*see also* democracies: evaluation of governments in; Internet: effect of, on democratic satisfaction); political activity and, 6; political confidence and, 6–7
Satisfaction with Democracy variable, 69
Saudi Arabia, women bloggers in, 36
secrecy, 7
selective exposure, theory of, 62
Shirky, Clay, 26, 135
Sina Weibo, 31–32
Singapore, elections in, Internet's effect on, 35–36
social constructionist view, 75, 109
social divide, 58
Social History of Media: From Gutenberg to the Internet, A (Briggs and Burke), 24
social network analysis, 36
sociotropic voting, 13
Sowore, Omoyele, 33
Stalin, Joseph, 25
Stiglitz, Joseph, 7
Stimson, James A., 70
Straits Times (Singapore), 36
survey instruments, shortfalls of, 17
Syria: conflict in, user-generated content and, 30; cyber warfare in, 54
Syrian Electronic Army, 54
systemic problems, political organization and, 136

Tanzania: general election in (2010), 4, 52, 113–14, 117–18; governmental institutions, trust in, 120–21; Internet users in, experiment findings of, 116–22; political information acquisition in, 39–40; press freedom in, 113; press in, trust of, 120; voting in, 121
Tanzania Election Monitoring Commission (TEMCO), 114
technology: convergence of, 60–62; impact of, debate over, 75
television, 25; censorship of, 36–37; gatekeepers of, 29; Internet compared to, 37; limitations of, 28–30; stories on, 28
time-series cross-sectional analysis, 69, 70, 74, 83
Tolbert, Caroline, 38, 49, 50, 58, 59
traditional media: censorship of, 36–37; limitations of, 26, 27; preferences of, 27; presenting different stories online, 29
transmission technologies, 23–24
transparency, for governments, 126
trust, Internet use and, 120–21
TSA (Transportation Security Administration), 30
Tunisia, 15
Twitter: blocked in China, 31; in Egypt, 32; in Saudi Arabia, 36; in Venezuela, 54
two-step flow theory of information, 59, 64

Uchaguzi TZ, 115
user-generated content, 30
Ushahidi, 114–15
U.S. State Department, 34

validity, 98
Venezuela, cyber warfare in, 53–54
Voice and Accountability indicator, 68
Voice of America, 40
VoIP (Voice over Internet Protocol), 60

weak democracies. *See* developing democracies
Wealth of Networks (Benkler), 140n1

WikiLeaks, 34
window-opening, 5, 21, 22, 40, 42, 47, 49–51, 104, 106; Arab Spring and, 12; Egyptian revolution and, 14–15; encouraging evaluations of governments, 50; limitations on, 53, 58, 63, 65; variations in, 128
wireless technology, 25

World Bank, 68
www.apologiesaccepted.com, 44, 45
www.sorryeverybody.com, 43–45

YouTube, 30, 33

Zaller, John, 8
Zetlen, James, 43